BALLOTS AND BANDWAGONS

CAMPAIGNS AND ELECTIONS

BALLOTS AND BANDWAGONS

CHOOSING THE CANDIDATES
by George Sullivan

CAMPAIGNS AND ELECTIONS
by George Sullivan

THE PRESIDENCY
by Richard M. Pious

CAMPAIGNS AND ELECTIONS

GEORGE SULLIVAN

Silver Burdett Press

Published by Silver Burdett Press, Inc., a division of Simon & Schuster, Inc.
Prentice Hall Bldg., Englewood Cliffs, NJ 07632.

Design by R^{studio} T.
Manufactured in the United States of America.

Lib. ed. 10 9 8 7 6 5 4 3 2 1

Paper ed. 10 9 8 7 6 5 4 3 2 1

Library of Congress Cataloging-in-Publication Data

Sullivan, George.
Campaigns and elections/George Sullivan.
p. cm. — (Ballots and bandwagons)
Includes bibliographical references and index.
Summary: Studies the history of American presidential campaign management,
showing the strategies and tactics the candidates have used over the decades to give
themselves positive exposure and their opponents negative exposure.
1. Elections — United States — History — Juvenile literature. 2. Electioneering —
United States — History — Juvenile literature. 3. Presidents — United States —
Election — History — Juvenile literature. [1. Elections — History. 2. Presidents —
Election — History. 3. Politics, Practical — History.] I. Title. II. Series.
JK1978, S85 1991
324, 973 — dc20   91-20403
                                                                                      CIP
                                                                                       AC

ISBN 0-382-24315-3   ISBN 0-382-24321-8 (paper)

CONTENTS

Massachusetts Governor Michael Dukakis reads from a teleprompter as he delivers a speech in Jersey City, New Jersey, during the 1988 presidential campaign.

CHAPTER ONE

MADE FOR TELEVISION

Every morning around 8 o'clock during the 1988 election campaign for the presidency of the United States, a management team for Vice-President George Bush, the Republican candidate, met in a downtown office in Washington, D.C., to make a decision on what the day's message should be. Top advisers to his Democratic opponent, Massachusetts governor Michael Dukakis, did the same.

Each day both candidates were flown to carefully selected locations with plenty of visual appeal. There they would speak for a strictly limited amount of time before a handpicked audience. Often there would be more reporters and television cameras than political supporters, but that was the point. The speeches were carefully tailored to put forward the theme of the day in short, simple, dramatic language.

At 6:30 in the evening, about ten hours after each candidate's advisers had planned the day's strategy, they would turn on their television sets to see whether the network newscasts had "correctly" carried their messages to the American public: George Bush is tough on crime. He is a patriot. He likes clean water. He will be the education president. Michael Dukakis loves America too. He won't cut Social Security benefits. He doesn't like guns very much.

This is "sound bite" politics. The term comes from the brief nine- or ten-second fragment that a television news editor "bites" out of a longer speech or event for broadcast. Commercial television time is expensive, and to make an impression in an affordable amount of time, television producers search for what is short, simple, direct, and provocative, within limits. Politicians know this, and by designing their remarks for the television format, they are often able to "manage" the news.

Of course, sound bites on the nightly news broadcasts are only one of the techniques candidates use to project their messages. There are also posters and billboards, newspaper and magazine advertisements, and radio and television commercials.

TV commercials—spot announcements, as they are called, or simply "spots"—are the chief means of reaching voters. Most are about thirty seconds in length. Such spots were the basic ingredient in the campaigns of Bush and Dukakis in 1988.

Though thirty seconds of paid television time may seem to give a political candidate greater scope than the nine- or ten-second sound bite, in practice both the sound bite and the spot use the same techniques of oversimplification and overstatement. The thirty-second spot has come in for heavy criticism because it is difficult to discuss a complex issue in such a brief amount of time. Seldom does the voter get any useful information from a thirty-second ad.

What is even worse is that spots and sound bites are frequently negative in tone. The candidates use them to attack one another. They are often filled with half-truths and distortions. The election of 1988 was said to have featured more negative advertising than any election in history.

Negative advertising was not invented in the 1980s. It has a long, rich history in American politics. But television has increased the visibility of negative advertising. A candidate's "attack ads" are repeated over and over in the living rooms of millions of Americans.

In the months following his election defeat in 1988, Michael Dukakis said he came to realize that he had made a big mistake in not fully understanding the power of negative campaigning and the television sound bite.

In a speech before the Civil Liberties Union of Hawaii in 1990, Dukakis declared that American democracy was being threatened by television. He stated, "I said in my acceptance speech at Atlanta that the 1988 election was not about ideology but about competence. I was wrong. It was about sound bites. And made-for-TV backdrops. And going negative."

The No-Issue Campaign

The biggest problem of the 1988 election campaign was the candidates' failure to come to grips with the issues of the day. The national debt was heading toward $3 trillion. The widespread use of drugs continued to fuel a national crime crisis. Banks were failing, environmental concerns were going unanswered, and the nation's urban centers could no longer provide minimally adequate services for their residents. A growing number of homeless wandered the streets of American cities.

There were important foreign policy matters to be dealt with as well. How was the new president going to deal with Mikhail Gorbachev and the Ayatollah Khomeini or with the collapsing economies of the Third World nations, or the rise of strong economic competitors in the Pacific?

New ideas and new policies were needed, but the two presidential candidates kept talking about patriotism, the American flag, prayer in the schools, and the Pledge of Allegiance. What we got, said political scientist Walter Dean Burnham, was "real junk food."

Changes in Campaigning

Running for president has changed enormously in the past fifty years. Every aspect of campaigning has been touched. The principal cause has been the *cost* of getting elected. Candidates must now

Documenting his patriotism, Vice-President George Bush addresses workers at a flag factory during the 1988 presidential campaign.

depend on the mass media — television, radio, newspapers, and magazines. Television, in particular, can reach tens of millions of people, but offers its time at rates that would shock the politicians of earlier generations.

Legal changes have affected how campaigns are financed and how money may be spent. In 1974 amendments to the Federal Election Campaign Act provided for public financing of presidential campaigns in an effort to ease a candidate's burden of raising money. The Federal Election Commission was created to enforce the rules and regulations of campaign financing.

But the sheer cost of the present system of campaigning can lead to corruption. Candidates continually sidestep the rules to raise ever increasing amounts of money — money that is spent largely to purchase television time.

These changes have helped to reduce the ideological influence of political parties. It is sometimes as difficult for Americans to determine what their political parties stand for as it is for those parties to sound out the wishes of the voters. Both major political parties have members who might be described as liberal or conservative, as well as those who change their views depending on how the wind blows. Many Americans view the two-party "machines" more as money-raising institutions than as groups that stand for particular principles, and today's voters are much more likely to vote on the basis of personal preference, or the issues, than because of a candidate's party affiliation.

With each recent election, television has grown in importance. Candidates appear on nightly newscasts and interview programs. They are featured in spot announcements. They appear in televised debates. Some two-thirds of the American voters now rely on TV for their information about the candidates and the issues. "Politics is show business," said Joe Klein in *New York* magazine during the presidential election year of 1988. *"Running for President* is a show that airs once a day in heartland America, just before *"Wheel of Fortune"* or the evening news."

The problem is that television, being a mass-market medium mainly designed to sell people products, has always searched for a message that will be agreeable to large numbers of people and offensive to as few as possible. Disturbing doubts, questions, and complexities will not sell toothpaste and detergents. Messages must be honed down to their simplest level and then constantly repeated. There is seldom any discussion of the issues, and little in the way of knowledge or enlightenment. It is no wonder that an increasing number of Americans are finding political campaigns irritating and boring. The evidence is that more thoughtful candidates are discouraged from running and voter turnout keeps declining.

On Election Day, 1988, a record 91 million Americans who could have voted did not. The turnout rate—50.16 percent of the eligible voters—was the lowest in a presidential election in this country in sixty-four years. The turnout rate was lower than in any other industrial democracy.

At the Republican National Convention in New Orleans in 1988, George Bush and Dan Quayle and their wives celebrate their nominations as president and vice-president. Months of election campaigning followed.

CHAPTER TWO

THE ELECTORAL COLLEGE

The main road to the White House is the presidential election, held every four years. Political parties choose their candidates through a long series of state caucuses, conventions, and primary elections, then formally nominate their selections at national conventions.

The election campaign follows—three hectic months in which the candidates must organize their staffs, raise money, plan strategy, and develop voter support.

On the first Tuesday after the first Monday in November, voters go to the polls. But they do not actually elect the president. Voters choose *electors*, whose votes elect the president. No other democracy in the world elects its leaders in quite the same way.

Looking Back

The system of electing electors came about because delegates at the Constitutional Convention held in Philadelphia in 1787 were unable to agree on a way to elect a president. Though

13

they had just fought a bloody war against the tyranny of England, not all the delegates at the convention were populists, or Jeffersonian democrats, as they have come to be called. Some were prosperous merchants and, like George Washington, wealthy farmers who feared the "mob" as much as King George did. They believed that only the educated and those who owned property were responsible enough to choose their leaders. These delegates opposed direct popular election and wanted the Congress to choose the president. Roger Sherman, a delegate from Connecticut, declared at the 1787 convention: "The people immediately should have as little to do as may be about the government. They want [lack] information and are constantly liable to be misled."

A compromise was reached in which each state would appoint a number of presidential electors equal to the total number of its senators and representatives in Congress. Each state, no matter how small it is in terms of population, has two senators and at least one member of the House of Representatives. Thus, every state has at least three electors. A heavily populated state has a large number of electors, equal to all its members in the House plus its two senators.

The body of electors from each state is called the electoral college. The word "college" has nothing to do with an institution of higher learning. In this case, it is a group of individuals. It is this group that, by simple majority vote, chooses the president. In practice, the names of electors are put forward by the political parties. If, for example, the candidate of the Democratic party wins the majority vote in a particular state, its slate of electors is chosen for the electoral college. Though these individuals are likely to vote for the Democratic presidential candidate, there is no constitutional requirement that they do so. As the founding fathers conceived the system, the electors are free to oppose the will of the "mob" if they wish.

Currently, there are 435 members of the House of Representatives and 100 members of the Senate plus 3 electoral votes from the District of Columbia. That is a total of 538, meaning that a presidential candidate must receive 270 electoral votes to be able to claim a majority. As the population of the United States increases or decreases or shifts from one state to another, the number of represen-

Electoral Votes for Each State
and the District of Columbia as of 1989

Alabama	9	Montana	3
Alaska	3	Nebraska	5
Arizona	8	Nevada	3
Arkansas	6	New Hampshire	4
California	47	New Jersey	17
Colorado	7	New Mexico	4
Connecticut	8	New York	38
Delaware	3	North Carolina	14
District of Columbia	3	North Dakota	3
Florida	20	Ohio	23
Georgia	14	Oklahoma	8
Hawaii	4	Oregon	6
Idaho	4	Pennsylvania	24
Illinois	24	Rhode Island	4
Indiana	13	South Carolina	8
Iowa	7	South Dakota	4
Kansas	6	Tennessee	10
Kentucky	9	Texas	30
Louisiana	10	Utah	4
Maine	4	Vermont	3
Maryland	10	Virginia	13
Massachusetts	13	Washington	9
Michigan	19	West Virginia	5
Minnesota	10	Wisconsin	10
Mississippi	7	Wyoming	3
Missouri	12	TOTAL:	538

tatives in the House changes, and therefore so does the number of electors permitted for each state.

The electors chosen by the voters in each state and the District of Columbia meet in their state capitals on the first Monday after the second Wednesday in December in election years to cast their ballots for president and vice-president. The ballots are sent under seal to the president of the Senate, who is the vice-president of the United States. Early in January the ballots are opened by the outgoing vice-president before a joint session of the newly elected Congress. "This announcement," the vice-president proclaims, "shall be deemed a sufficient declaration of the persons elected president and vice-president of the United States."

In January 1989, in an unusual twist of history, it happened that George Bush, then vice-president, was the one who announced that candidate George Bush had been elected president of the United States. The electoral vote was 426 for Bush, 111 for Michael Dukakis, and 1 for Lloyd Bentsen, who had been Dukakis's vice-presidential running mate.

The opposite situation occurred in January 1968, when Hubert Humphrey, the outgoing vice-president, had the rather somber task of announcing that Richard Nixon, who had defeated him in the previous November election, was the new president. Nixon must have known how Humphrey felt. Nixon was vice-president in 1960 and had to announce *his* defeat at the hands of John F. Kennedy.

Winner Take All

The Constitution leaves it to the states to decide how to award their electoral votes. Forty-nine states now award *all* their electors to the candidate who gets a majority of the popular vote. Maine, however, awards two electors to the statewide winner in the popular vote and one vote to the winner of each of the state's two congressional districts. As an example of what happens in every state but Maine, look at the results of the popular vote in California in 1988. It was fairly close:

George Bush   5,054,917
Michael Dukakis   4,702,233

That meant that George Bush, having won the popular vote, was awarded all 47 of California's electoral votes. Dukakis, despite the fact that almost five million Californians voted for him, received no electoral votes from the state. In this type of winner-take-all system, the general election comes down to forty-nine separate state contests plus one in the District of Columbia.

Problems

The electoral college has not always worked very well. In several elections the candidate having the largest popular vote was defeated.

In 1824 Andrew Jackson won the popular vote but lost the election. The electoral vote went like this:

Andrew Jackson	99
John Quincy Adams	84
William Crawford	41
Henry Clay	37

If no candidate has a majority of the electoral votes, the Constitution leaves it to the House of Representatives to choose a president from among the top three candidates through a simple majority vote, with each state having only one vote, regardless of the number of its representatives. Henry Clay, the Speaker of the House and a longtime foe of Jackson, was out of the running, and threw his support to Adams. That gave Adams a majority of the votes and he was named president. After his inauguration, Adams appointed Clay secretary of state. As a result, charges of corruption were leveled at Adams throughout his presidency.

In the 1876 election the popular Samuel J. Tilden, a Democrat, defeated Republican Rutherford B. Hayes by more than a quarter of a million votes, 4,284,757 to 4,033,950. But don't look for Tilden's name on any list of American presidents.

Neither of the candidates received the then-required majority of 185 electoral votes. Tilden had 184; Hayes had 165. Twenty votes were in dispute, nineteen of them from Florida, Louisiana, and South Carolina. An extraordinary Electoral Commission was set up to end the deadlock. The commission consisted of five senators, five

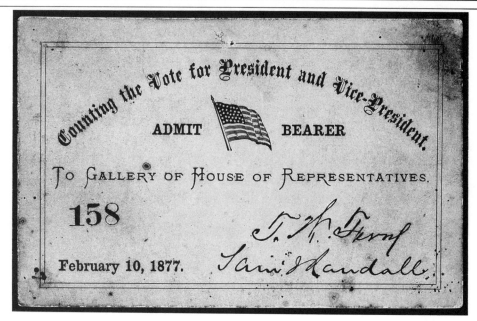

In the election of 1876, neither candidate received the required number of electoral votes, which led to special vote counting by an Electoral Commission.

representatives, and five Supreme Court justices. Seven of them were Republicans; seven were Democrats; Justice Joseph Bradley ended up as the fifteenth member. Bradley was expected to be nonpartisan, but he voted with the Republicans on every important issue. The result was that by a vote of eight to seven, the Electoral Commission handed all the disputed electoral votes to Hayes, giving him 185 votes to Tilden's 184. Many Democrats grumbled about a "stolen election." But they agreed to accept the decision of the commission in return for promises that Hayes would remove federal troops from Louisiana and South Carolina, appoint at least one Southerner to his cabinet, and support federal aid for education and internal improvements in the South.

In 1888 the system broke down a third time. Benjamin Harrison became president by earning 233 electoral votes to 168 for Grover Cleveland. But Cleveland had 90,000 more popular votes than Harrison (5,540,050 to 5,444,337). What happened was that Harrison won by slim margins in several states, enough to pick up the required number of electoral votes. Cleveland won other states by big majorities, rolling up more popular votes than his rival.

Breaking a Tie

Another potential problem with the electoral college lies with the present number of electors—538. Since it is an even number, a tie in the voting is always possible. Were each candidate to wind up with 269 electoral votes, the House of Representatives would be required to choose the president. A majority of 26 states would have to cast their votes for one candidate.

Great turmoil would surely result, especially in states that happened to be about equal in Democratic and Republican representation. Or it could happen that the 26 smallest states, with only 22 percent of the population, could, with their 26 votes, elect the president.

A tie almost occurred in 1976, when Republican Gerald Ford faced Democrat Jimmy Carter, the eventual winner. Had Ford won in Ohio, a state he lost by 11,000 votes out of the approximately 4 million cast, and in Delaware, which he lost by 13,000 out of 230,000 cast, he would have had 269 electoral votes. Carter's total also would have been 269. The House of Representatives would have been called upon to decide the outcome.

There is a simple solution to this problem. The size of the House of Representatives, now set at 435 members, could be changed by one, to either 436 or 434 members. The 103 electors, based upon the 100 senators and the 3 electors from the District of Columbia, added to 436 or 434, would result in an uneven number of electors. There could be no tie. The Constitution grants Congress the power to determine the size of the House of Representatives. In the 1920s the number of members was set at 435. It could be changed.

Breaking Faith

Another problem with the electoral college is that the electors are not compelled to vote for their party's nominees. And some have

President Gerald Ford poses with baseball star Pete Rose as he campaigns in Ohio in 1976. Had Ford won the state's electoral votes, and those of Delaware, he would have won the election.

not. They have violated the trust placed in them by the voters and supported someone else. Such free exercise of the will has yet to influence the outcome of an election, but it could happen someday.

The Constitution does not require electors to vote for their party's choice for president and vice-president. It requires only that at least one of the persons for whom the elector votes, in separate ballots for president and vice-president, must not live in that elector's home state. In some states, electors are "pledged" to vote for the candidates named by the party. But pledged or not, the voters assume that each elector will carry out their mandate.

What happens when an elector votes for someone other than the winner of a state's popular vote? Nothing can be done. The vote is counted as cast. Following the 1988 presidential election, the electoral vote was 426 for George Bush, 111 for Michael Dukakis, and 1 for Lloyd Bentsen. The single vote for Bentsen, the Democratic senator from Texas who was Dukakis's vice-presidential running mate, was cast by Margarette Leach, an elector from West Virginia.

Leach, who was also vice-president of the West Virginia Federation of Democratic Women, said, "I wanted to make a statement about the electoral college. We've outgrown it. And I wanted to point up what I perceive as a weakness in the system—that 270 people can get together in this country and elect a president, whether he's on the ballot or not."

Hardly an election passes without at least one elector doing what he or she wants. In 1976 Governor Ronald Reagan of California received one vote from an elector from the state of Washington. Reagan was not nominated for the presidency until 1980, four years later. In 1972 a Republican elector from Virginia cast his vote for the Libertarian party candidates, John Hosper and Theodora Nathan. The vice-presidential electoral vote for Theodora Nathan was the first electoral vote ever cast for a woman.

In 1960, when Democratic candidate John F. Kennedy was elected president, a serious split over civil rights occurred among Democratic electors in Alabama and Mississippi, who ran unpledged. A total of fifteen electors ended up casting their votes for Harry F. Byrd, rejecting Kennedy, the party's nominee.

Students of the electoral system worry that in some future election one or more electors might spurn the people's choice to vote for someone else, thus triggering a constitutional crisis. They have suggested that we continue the electoral system as it is but do away with the electoral college. In other words, the candidate winning the majority of the state's popular vote would get all the state's electoral votes automatically. There would be no meeting of electors, no casting of ballots. There then would be no opportunity for an elector to ignore the choice of his or her party, and vote for some other candidate. While the role of electors in presidential elections keeps being challenged, few suggest sending them into retirement.

Direct Elections
Everytime there is a presidential election, proposals are put forward for doing away with the electoral college. The idea heard most often is that the president should be elected by simple popular vote. Whichever candidate gets the most votes nationwide wins. Direct

Jessie Jackson campaigned for the Democratic nomination in 1988—and lost. Under a system of direct elections, he might have formed a third party and entered the race for the presidency.

election, as this is called, seems democratic, but it is not without some flaws of its own.

Under the present electoral system, each state is recognized as a vital part of the election process. Even the smallest states in terms of population, such as Delaware, Utah, and Wyoming, have at least three electors each (two for their two senators and one for their member of the House of Representatives).

With direct election of the president, the role of the smaller states would be diminished. Candidates would concentrate on the heavily populated states. They do now, of course, but direct election would increase their tendency to do so.

Another criticism of direct elections is that they would encourage the formation of third parties, and even fourth and fifth parties. New political parties are free to organize under the present system, but it is difficult for any one of them to win a majority of a state's popular votes and thereby earn that state's electoral votes. When John Anderson ran as an independent candidate in 1980, opposing Democrat Jimmy Carter and Republican Ronald Reagan, he got almost six million popular votes—but not a single electoral vote.

In the case of a direct election, however, every party on the ballot would get the votes cast for it. With the vote split among several different candidates, the result could easily be the election of a president who received less than a majority of the votes cast. Such a system would lead to the creation of many different political parties with narrow interests, and this would not be healthy for the nation. With only two major parties, a presidential candidate must appeal to a wide range of Americans in order to win. He or she must demonstrate acceptability to voters with a variety of social, economic, and geographic backgrounds. A candidate who appeals only to the rich or poor, to business, to farmers, to organized labor, to a particular ethnic group, to the Northeast or to the Deep South would find it almost impossible to be elected. Under a two-party system, one or the other of the candidates is virtually guaranteed the support of the majority of the voters, and this contributes to the stability of our government. But with a multiparty system, a candidate representing a special interest would have a much better chance of winning.

That's a chief reason why direct elections have not won wider support from the major political parties.

Changing the System

Changing the electoral system is possible only by amending the Constitution. This can be done in two ways. The first is to convene a constitutional convention. The alternative, which is more common, is for two-thirds of the membership of both houses of Congress to vote in favor of the change, after which the amendment must be approved by three-quarters of the states.

A proposed constitutional amendment to abolish the electoral college and replace it with direct elections reached the Senate floor in 1979. The Senate voted in favor of the measure, 51 to 48, but that was 15 votes short of the two-thirds majority needed. All the same, it is quite clear that more than a few legislators believe the nation may have outgrown the electoral college.

As it is now, if a state favors a candidate by only a tiny number of votes, that candidate wins the entire electoral vote of the state. The opposing candidate, who may have polled almost as many votes, gets no electors. His or her popular vote, which could run into millions, counts for nothing. This system of awarding electoral votes troubles some people. They feel it is unfair and should be changed.

In 1972, Maine, with four electoral votes, abandoned the system. As mentioned earlier, Maine awards one vote to a presidential candidate for each congressional district he or she carries. The two other votes go to whichever candidate wins the popular vote statewide. The lower houses of the legislatures of Connecticut and North Carolina have passed bills that would do away with the winner-take-all system and distribute electoral votes the way Maine does. New Jersey and Louisiana are said to be considering such changes.

Those who support the Maine system of allocating electoral votes say it would increase candidates' interest in many states and thereby boost voter participation. Under the current system, the outcome in many states is pretty well known several weeks before the voters go to the polls. A candidate, believing that he or she cannot win a majority in a particular state, and will therefore lose *all* its electoral votes, may decide not to campaign at all in that state. Interest in the election dwindles as a result.

This happened in Florida during the 1988 presidential election. By the second week of September, two months before election day, Michael Dukakis realized that he had only the slimmest chance of winning the state, and shut down operations there. But there are eight Florida districts that generally vote Democratic in national elections. Under the winner-take-all system, Dukakis had no reason to campaign in those districts. Even if he had won all eight districts, he still would have lost the state. But under the system used in Maine, Dukakis would have had an incentive to try for those votes.

Such a reform would also benefit third parties. If a minor-party candidate could win enough state election districts, even if he or she could not win the majority of those districts, there would still be a chance of winning electoral votes. Such a showing could thus have an impact on the national election, or at least avert having one's voter strength disappear completely.

But suppose a proportional system were installed in place of what we now have. Minor parties, winning as little as 5 or 10 percent of the vote, could deny a majority to one of the major party candidates. A minor party with a radical left-wing or right-wing program could hold the balance of power as the two major parties bargained for support. Israel is one nation to have experienced the failings of a multiparty system. In recent years, awkward alliances between large and small parties have led to ineffective government in that country.

Except for occasional lapses, the electoral college system, the winner-take-all system, has worked well for nearly 200 years. And the systems that have been proposed to replace it are known to be filled with risk.

CHAPTER THREE

LOG CABINS, HARD CIDER, AND COONSKIN CAPS

The political campaign that pitted George Bush against Michael Dukakis in 1988 was said to be a nasty one, filled with factual distortions and personal attacks. "Pigsty politics" was what the *Washington Post* called it. Some people blamed television and the new generation of media professionals, who were experts at creating the provocative, unanswerable catchphrase. But television did not create dirty campaigns. They are a tradition of long standing, as American as apple pie.

Though there have been great changes in campaign technology in recent decades, the essential ingredients are pretty much the same as they were in the 1820s. Instead of television commercials to promote their cause, candidates relied on different types of printed material — newspapers, handbills, pamphlets, and posters (or broadsides, as they were called). For color and excitement, there was the torchlight parade. A candidate's supporters, numbering anywhere from a few hundred to several thousand, marched through the streets shouting and

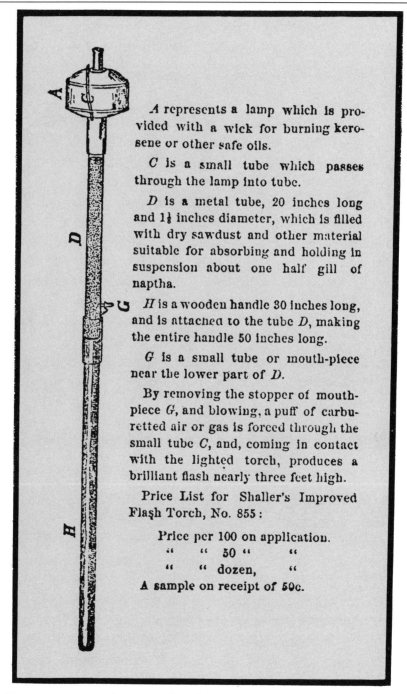

A represents a lamp which is provided with a wick for burning kerosene or other safe oils.

C is a small tube which passes through the lamp into tube.

D is a metal tube, 20 inches long and 1½ inches diameter, which is filled with dry sawdust and other material suitable for absorbing and holding in suspension about one half gill of naptha.

H is a wooden handle 30 inches long, and is attached to the tube *D*, making the entire handle 50 inches long.

G is a small tube or mouth-piece near the lower part of *D*.

By removing the stopper of mouth-piece *G*, and blowing, a puff of carburetted air or gas is forced through the small tube *C*, and, coming in contact with the lighted torch, produces a brilliant flash nearly three feet high.

Price List for Shaller's Improved Flash Torch, No. 855:

Price per 100 on application.
"   "   50 "   "
"   "   dozen,   "
A sample on receipt of 50c.

For use in campaign parades, this torch had a special feature that enabled it to produce a "brilliant flash nearly three feet high."

carrying burning torches. It was exciting and dramatic, a high point of the campaign for those who took part or witnessed it.

Candidates were also boosted by political rallies. In some towns, the rally was an important social event as well as a political happening, requiring many weeks of preparation. Rallies were often held in auditoriums or ballparks. Bands played; sometimes there were fireworks. Often the rally had the flavor of a carnival or a county fair. The high point of the rally was the appearance of the candidate and his speech.

Even the campaign speech was a radical departure from the earliest elections, where those who wanted to be president, or incumbents seeking a second term, did not deliver campaign speeches. The earliest presidential candidates believed that the office should seek the person; the person should not seek the office. It was, at least publicly, considered undignified to seek the presidency.

That began to change with the election of 1828, a contest between the incumbent President John Quincy Adams and General Andrew Jackson, a military hero of the War of 1812. Each had a different view about campaigning. Adams, in the tradition of George Washington, insisted on doing little or nothing on his own behalf. "If my country wants me," he said, "she must ask for me." Overtly, Adams took the high road, though it may have been haughtiness rather than principle.

Jackson did nothing in public to break with the tradition established by Washington, but he worked hard behind the scenes to build a campaign organization and plan strategy.

The Adams forces, attempting to discredit Jackson, printed a handbill that has become a classic in the annals of campaign "dirty tricks." The handbill concerned six soldiers, one a Baptist minister, who had been convicted of desertion and executed, with Jackson's approval, during the Creek War in Alabama in 1813. The handbill portrayed the soldiers as innocent men who had completed their service and merely wanted to go home. It claimed that Jackson had murdered them in cold blood.

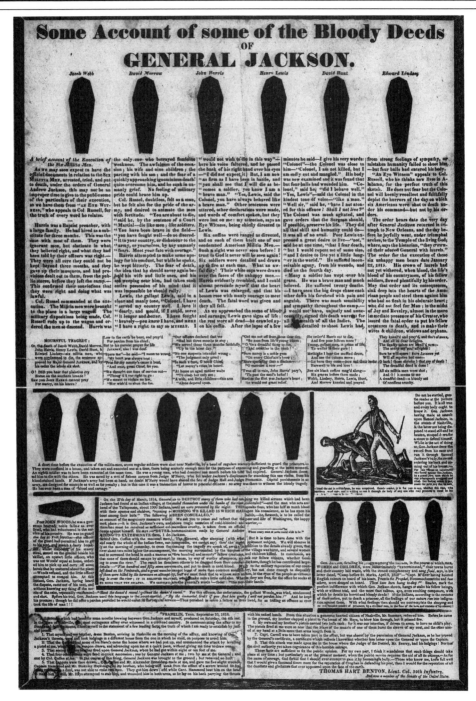

Coffin handbills like this one helped John Quincy Adams defeat Andrew Jackson in the election of 1828.

The handbill's headline read: SOME ACCOUNT OF SOME OF THE BLOODY DEEDS OF GENERAL JACKSON. Bordered in black, the handbill pictured six coffins, one for each of the soldiers.

The "coffin handbill," as it came to be called, infuriated the Jackson forces. They did their best to tell what really happened in 1813. At the time, Jackson's campaign against the Indians was at a critical stage. The six soldiers in question had broken into a military storehouse, stolen supplies, burned a bakehouse, and then deserted. After their capture, they had been given fair trials; their rights had not been violated.

During the campaign, Jackson was also characterized as a gambler, bigamist, slave trader, drunkard, thief, and liar. But he was immensely popular and managed to overcome such attacks—and the "coffin handbill"—to defeat Adams. Jackson and his followers called the victory a "triumph of the great principles of self-government." By 1828 many states had eliminated the ownership of property as a qualification for voting, and many less wealthy Americans were voting for the first time. For this reason, the patrician Adams and his backers looked upon Jackson's victory as the triumph of the masses.

Image Building

The Constitution makes no mention of political parties, much less the important role they now play in the nomination and election of the president. But political parties were beginning to take shape even before George Washington became the nation's first president in 1789. Two groups with common economic and political interests formed the first political parties, the Federalist party and the Democratic-Republican party. Both of these parties split apart after the 1816 presidential election. By 1828 the remnants of the Federalists became the National Republicans, who had put forward Adams as their candidate. Jackson was supported by a faction of the Democratic-Republicans. That became, simply, Democrats.

In the election of 1832, Andrew Jackson again overwhelmingly defeated the candidate of the National Republicans, Henry Clay,

This cartoon from the election of 1828 was used to remind voters of Jackson's executions of army deserters. The caption read: "Jackson is to be President and you will be HANGED."

For the election of 1840, William Henry Harrison, of well-to-do background, was transformed into the log cabin candidate — plain, simple, and down-to-earth.

and the National Republicans were politically bankrupted. Opposition to Jackson began to center around a new group, the Whig party. The term is short for *whiggamore*, used to describe a band of seventeenth-century Scottish rebels. The new Whig party hoped to cloak itself in the image of those who were against a tyrannical king, that is, Jackson. They represented a variety of disaffected groups, but generally favored a high protective tariff, to help domestic industries, and economic expansion, while opposing the strength of the presidency.

Through the 1830s, political parties were refining their campaign techniques and holding state and national nominating conventions to generate mass enthusiasm for their candidates. In 1840, with political parties organized throughout the states, a full-fledged election campaign was held for the first time. The election of 1840 had many modern features. It pitted incumbent President Martin Van Buren, a Democrat, against William Henry Harrison, a Whig.

Harrison was the son of a wealthy Virginia planter. He had gone to college, enlisted in the army, and risen to the rank of major general. He later became a representative and a senator from Ohio. At the time he was nominated for the presidency, he and his family were living on their estate in North Bend, Ohio.

The Whigs launched an all-out campaign to win the support of the masses, seeking to sell Harrison as a "people's candidate." It did not matter to the Whigs that Harrison was well-to-do and college educated or that his military career had been less than notable. As governor of the Indiana Territory, Harrison had led forces that took part in a battle against the Shawnee Indians at Tippecanoe in 1811. After blunting an Indian attack, Harrison's men destroyed the Indian village, while suffering heavy casualties. Nevertheless, in what today would be called image building, the Whigs hailed Harrison as "the hero of Tippecanoe." Since John Tyler of Virginia was Harrison's running mate, the slogan "Tippecanoe and Tyler too," was created.

The Whigs presented Harrison as being plain and down-to-earth. He was characterized as the "farmer of North Bend," born in a log cabin, a man who had worked hard to get ahead. His tastes and

This campaign bandanna from the election of 1840 features Harrison's log-cabin, hard-cider theme.

habits were said to be those of an ordinary citizen. He drank hard cider, not the French champagne favored by Van Buren. Log cabins, coonskin caps, and hard cider became Whig campaign symbols.

Whig rallies often attracted tens of thousands of spectators, and their parades stretched for miles. Whig log cabins were erected in every city and town in the country, from which hard cider — or sweet cider, for teetotalers — was dispensed. Log cabins were carried in parades and pictured on banners and bandannas. There were log cabin sunbonnets, log cabin buttons, log cabin teacups, log cabin plates, and log cabin songbooks. There was Tippecanoe Tobacco and Tippecanoe Shaving Soap. The Whigs also produced metal tokens, each about the size of a quarter, picturing log cabins or bottles of hard cider. These tokens were the precursor of the modern campaign button.

The Whigs made much of the slogan "Keep the ball rolling." They created huge Harrison balls, ten or twelve feet in diameter, made of twine, paper, leather, or tin, plastered them with campaign slogans, and then rolled them through city streets or from town to town. As the balls rolled, the people chanted:

What has caused this great commotion, motion, motion,
Our country through?
It is the ball a-rolling on,
For Tippecanoe and Tyler, too, Tippecanoe and
Tyler, too.

Women were not permitted to vote in those days but many hundreds of them supported Harrison's cause. They made speeches, rode on parade floats, and marched with brooms to "sweep" the Democrats out of office. A Whig newspaper stated that "if the ladies only were entitled to vote, Old Tip [for Tippecanoe] would be swept into office."

The Democrats countered that no one knew Harrison's position on any of the critical issues of the day, whereas Van Buren's policies as president were well known. When it came to the issues, the Democrats called Harrison "General Mum." They also charged that Harrison was not mentally or physically qualified to be president.

Harrison responded by making a series of speeches on his own behalf, becoming the first presidential candidate to do so. The central issue of the day had to do with economics. Not long after Van Buren had taken office, the nation was struck by the Panic of 1837, the worst depression in American history up to that time. Van Buren failed to react effectively to what had happened.

But Harrison's speeches avoided important economic or social issues. He followed the advice of Nicholas Biddle, president of the

Bank of the United States, who had told Whig leaders: "Let him not say one single word about his principles, or his creed—let him say nothing—promise nothing. Let no Committee or Convention, no town meeting, ever extract from him a single word about what he thinks now, or what he will do hereafter."

Harrison's speechmaking showed that a candidate could campaign actively for the presidency without suffering a loss of honor or esteem. Nevertheless, in the presidential campaigns that immediately followed, there was no great rush by candidates to speak out. Such behavior was still considered to be improper.

Some 2.4 million people turned out to vote, about twice the number that had voted in 1832. An estimated 80 percent of the voters went to the polls. When the votes were counted, Harrison emerged as a clear winner. He got 1,275,017 popular votes to Van Buren's 1,128,702. Harrison won 234 electoral votes to Van Buren's 60. The excitement that the Whigs had generated had carried the day.

The Harrison victory showed that a presidential election campaign did not have to deal with serious issues at all. It could be a popularity contest. The Whigs had transformed Harrison from a Virginia aristocrat into a log-cabin dwelling, hard-cider drinking common man, and had stolen from Van Buren and his Jacksonian Democrats their populist image. Image making had worked.

The Democrats were infuriated by the methods the Whigs had used to gain their victory. They were still steaming four years later when they sat down to write their party platform, putting in it a plank that condemned "facetious symbolism and displays insulting to the judgment and subversive to the intellect of the people." But party platforms never have had much influence on the nation's social and political customs, and the Democratic platform of 1844 was no exception.

Lincoln and Douglas, 1860

But the old, more modest style of campaigning died a slow death. As late as 1860, Abraham Lincoln was still able to wage an election campaign from his front porch in Illinois. In May of that year, Lincoln captured the Republican nomination for the presidency. The Republican party had come into existence through a series of antislavery meetings held in the north in the 1850s. Meanwhile, the Whigs broke into sectional groups, with the Northern Whigs joining the Republicans. The Democrats chose Stephen A. Douglas.

Lincoln followed the old campaign tradition and remained in Springfield, Illinois, where he continued to work as a lawyer. There he received a stream of visitors, including friends, politicians, and reporters. He made no speeches.

Douglas, however, hit the campaign trail, becoming the first presidential candidate in history to tour the nation in person. His decision to campaign actively shocked many citizens. But Douglas, who believed that the citizens should be allowed to vote on the issue of slavery, felt he had to take his case to the people.

With Lincoln at home, noted Republicans appeared in Northern cities on his behalf. The Republicans sponsored barbecues and rallies, and formed bands of young men called "Wide Awakes," who, at 6 feet 4 inches were as tall as Lincoln. In capes and helmets, the "Wide Awakes" snake-danced under torchlights in several Northern cities. So the fact that the presidential candidate stayed at home did not mean that the election lacked excitement and color. Since many voters of the time cast their national ballots on the basis of regional issues, as put forward by local party functionaries, the presence of Lincoln was not demanded.

In any case, the issues in 1860 were of overwhelming importance: the extension of slavery to new territories; states' rights versus the powers of the national government; and the question of secession. And two years before the presidential election, in an Illinois senatorial campaign, Lincoln and Douglas had already probed these issues in a series of seven famous face-to-face debates. So the views of the candidates were well known. Lincoln, incidentally, lost the Senate seat but is considered to have performed brilliantly and beaten Douglas in the debates.

Lincoln won a majority of electoral votes in the presidential election and got 1,866,352 popular votes, about 40 percent of the total.

A Mathew Brady photo of Abraham Lincoln, taken during the presidential campaign of 1860. Lincoln followed tradition and campaigned from his home in Springfield, Illinois. In contrast, the Democratic candidate, Stephen Douglas, toured the nation.

More Dirty Tricks

For the election of 1884 the Republicans offered James G. Blaine from Maine, a former congressman and secretary of state. Charming and often funny, skilled and experienced as a campaigner, Blaine would have been a heavy favorite except for one failing—his name and that of his vice-presidential running mate, John A. Logan, had been linked to shady financial dealings. His opponents called Blaine "Slippery Jim."

The Democratic nominee was New York's portly, dignified governor, Grover Cleveland, a lawyer who had been mayor of Buffalo. Cleveland, known as "Grover the Good" because he was so honest, did little campaigning, preferring to remain at work at the governor's office in Albany. Blaine, on the other hand, spent several weeks touring the country, ridiculing Cleveland for his lack of experience.

Late in July 1884, a front-page story in the *Buffalo Telegraph* appeared under a headline that read: A TERRIBLE TALE; A DARK CHAPTER IN A PUBLIC MAN'S HISTORY. The story revealed that Cleveland was the father of an out-of-wedlock son, 10 years old at the time. The boy's mother was a thirty-six-year-old Buffalo widow. Cleveland, the story said, had been providing both with financial aid. Cleveland did not deny the story. When his campaign manager asked him how the situation should be handled, Cleveland answered, "Whatever you say, tell the truth."

Newspapers of the day called Cleveland a "gross and licentious man," "a moral leper," and described him as being "worse in moral quality than a pickpocket." The president of Amherst College told students that only voters with corrupt morals could support Cleveland. Republicans chanted: "Ma! Ma! Where's my Pa? Gone to the White House. Hah! Hah! Hah!"

The Republicans had their troubles, too. A letter turned up with new evidence connecting Blaine to scandalous financial dealings. The Democrats reproduced the letter and distributed it far and wide. And at party rallies, people were encouraged to chant:

> Blaine! Blaine!
> The Continental liar
> From the State of Maine!

OUR NEXT PRESIDENT

"Slippery Jim" is what his opponents called James J. Blaine, the Republican presidential candidate in 1884.

The election was very close, with Cleveland winning by only 62,683 out of the almost ten million votes that were cast (4,911,017 to 4,848,334). Cleveland got 219 electoral votes, Blaine, 182.

As the turn of the century approached, most of the elements that would make up the modern presidential campaign were in place. Presidential candidates were coming to accept the need for active campaigning. All that was lacking was the technology that would enable candidates to project their messages to the public at large. That technology was soon to become available.

CHAPTER FOUR

WHISTLE STOPPING

From the second half of the nineteenth century, when most presidential candidates abandoned the stay-at-home "front porch" campaign, until the introduction and widespread use of television and computers in the 1960s, it was important for someone seeking the presidency to be seen and heard in person by as many voters as possible. Candidates found faster and more efficient ways to travel.

Stephen A. Douglas, when he ran for United States senator from Illinois against Abraham Lincoln in 1858, is credited with conducting the first whistle-stop campaign tour by train. To let the people of a town know that his train had arrived at their station, Douglas would fire a cannon that was carried on a flatcar.

The campaign train was a special world on wheels. It was usually twelve to eighteen cars in length, with individual cars for the candidate and his staff. There was a dining car, of course, and sleeping cars.

There was also a separate car for the press, which was often located in the middle of the train.

Franklin D. Roosevelt, campaigning for the presidency in September 1932, holds a press conference as his private train passes through Ohio.

Typically, it was an ordinary passenger car that had been stripped of seats and fitted out with long tables for rows of typewriters.

At one end of the press car was an office for the Western Union representative. His job was to collect the reporters' stories and drop them off at telegraph stations along the way, so they could be transmitted to the newspapers. If the train did not stop at a station, the Western Union man would put the reporters' stories in a weighted bag and hurl it at the stationmaster as the train sped through.

At the other end of the press car was a darkroom for the use of photographers. In his 1928 campaign for the presidency, Democratic candidate Al Smith introduced duplicating equipment to print advance copies of his speeches for reporters.

At each stop the candidate would step out onto the open platform at the rear of the last car and make a short speech, almost always the same one. Only the name of the local town and local politicians changed. Sometimes several thousand people would show up to hear the candidate. At other times there might be only a hundred or so. In 1920 Warren G. Harding had loudspeakers installed at the rear of the train.

At each stop, reporters would scramble from the train and gather at the rear to observe the size of the crowd and gauge the reaction to the candidate's speech, and to see whether the candidate might say anything new. They had to keep alert or the train would pull out without them. President Franklin D. Roosevelt, in particular, insisted that the train start at the very moment he ceased speaking. He would bring his speech to a rousing climax, and then the train would pull out as the crowd cheered and Roosevelt waved back at them. It was very dramatic.

Perfecting the Art

The campaign train came of age during the lively presidential campaign of 1896, which was about money. It was called the "Battle of Standards." Democrat William Jennings Bryan, a handsome young Nebraskan with a magnificent voice, favored the free and unlimited coinage of silver. His opponent, Republican William McKinley, was a "goldbug." McKinley upheld the gold standard, believing that gold should be used to back the nation's monetary system. The real issue here was the free expansion of the money supply and the availability of easy credit, or loans, to people with no capital, or savings. The use of the gold standard favored the big banks, railroads, wealthy industrialists, and emerging monopolies, whereas the free coinage of silver meant easy loans for the "common man."

Bryan versus McKinley thus became a battle of the West and South against the East, debtor versus creditor, farmer versus industrialist, and the poor and underprivileged versus the rich.

McKinley and his supporters were very confident. Bryan, at thirty-six, was very young to be a presidential candidate. He was barely old enough to meet the age requirement of thirty-five set by

Democrat William Jennings Bryan, a presidential candidate in 1896, 1900, and again in 1906, pioneered the art of whistle stopping.

This postcard from the early 1900s attests to Bryan's reputation as a fervent and long-winded speaker.

the Constitution. And, coming from Nebraska, he did not, in terms of electoral votes, represent an important state. His campaign was hampered by poor organization and a lack of money. But Bryan was a magnificent speaker, and he understood the art of whistle-stop campaigning. He traveled some 18,000 miles by train and made speeches by the hundreds, sometimes as many as ten or twenty in a day. He visited twenty-seven states and addressed some five million people.

Even in the middle of the night, men and women clustered about his train at stops or crowded railroad stations in the hope of hearing him. Crowds of 25,000 to 50,000 people were common. When he was charged with lacking dignity for campaigning so openly, Bryan replied, ". . . I would rather have it said that I lacked dignity than . . . that I lack backbone to meet the enemies of the government who work against its welfare on Wall Street."

While Bryan traveled the country, McKinley acted in a much more traditional fashion, conducting a "front porch" campaign from his home in Canton, Ohio. His campaign manager arranged for thousands of visitors. Once a delegation had arrived in McKinley's front yard, a spokesman would make a short address. McKinley would then respond with a brief speech of his own, which was widely reported by the press.

In the campaign's final stages, McKinley and his backers became alarmed by the amount of support Bryan seemed to be attracting, but in the end the Republican candidate prevailed. Almost 14 million voters went to the polls, giving 7,035,638 popular votes to McKinley and 6,467,946 votes to Bryan. In the electoral voting, McKinley won by 271 to 176.

McKinley and Bryan were opposing candidates a second time four years later. But in 1900 they had to share the stage with the colorful Theodore Roosevelt, who ran as vice-president on the Republican ticket. Roosevelt was just as energetic as Bryan. He traveled 21,000 miles, speaking in hundreds of cities and towns. Once again the voters chose McKinley. But six months after the inauguration, William McKinley was assassinated, and Theodore Roosevelt became president.

Breaking New Ground

James G. Blaine had campaigned in 1884 and William Jennings Bryan had whistle-stopped far and wide in 1896. Both Bryan and Theodore Roosevelt were active campaigners in 1900. William Howard Taft had done some speechmaking in 1908, when he won election as the twenty-seventh president. But none of these candidates was president at the time. The belief still prevailed that it was undignified and improper for an incumbent president to deliver campaign speeches. Even in 1904, when President Theodore Roosevelt, always a bold and spirited figure, was seeking reelection, he stuck loyally to tradition, and did not campaign. But from his home in Oyster Bay on Long Island in New York State, Roosevelt set campaign strategy and tactics. He also corresponded constantly with party leaders in every section of the country and with his cabinet

When William Howard Taft hit the campaign trail in 1912, he became the first presidential candidate to speak out on his own behalf.

secretaries, urging them to do battle against the Democrats. Roosevelt scored a smashing victory.

The tradition of non-campaigning finally came to an end in 1912. William Howard Taft, who sought reelection that year, was bitterly angry at Theodore Roosevelt, one of his two rivals, who, after failing in his attempt to win the Republican nomination, ran as the Progressive party candidate. Roosevelt had been a frequent critic of the Taft administration. Taft was likewise disturbed by Roosevelt's politics, which he considered to be a bit too liberal. "Whether I win or lose is not the important thing," Taft told journalist Charles Thompson. "I am in this fight to perform a great public duty—the duty of keeping Theodore Roosevelt out of the White House."

Though Taft broke new ground by hitting the campaign trail, he failed to campaign enough. He did not seem to have the heart for it. "Sometimes, I think I might as well give up as far as being a candidate is concerned," he wrote. "There are so many people out there who don't like me."

Democrat Woodrow Wilson was the third candidate. An effective campaigner, Wilson impressed audiences with his serious-minded speeches and occasional humor. Unlike Taft or Roosevelt, Wilson refused to deal in personalities. Wilson won, and Roosevelt finished second. Taft took his defeat in stride. "I have one consolation," he said. "No one candidate was ever elected ex-president by so large a majority."

Victory for an Underdog

President Harry Truman, who assumed the office when Franklin Roosevelt died in 1945, made what became a famous whistle-stop campaign in 1948, when he was struggling to win a full term in the White House. Truman's opponent was New York Governor Thomas E. Dewey. Most political experts believed that Dewey was going to win. Dewey thought he was going to win, too. At one point during the campaign, he took time out to plan his inauguration.

At a point when candidates were beginning to take an interest in television, Truman took a step back in time by launching a whistle-stop campaign. The "Truman Special," as it was called, was a train of sixteen cars that was home to Truman and his family, about a hundred news reporters, speechwriters and other campaign staff members, and Secret Service agents. It traveled some 25,000 miles.

On some days Truman would make as many as twenty speeches. He was friendly, forthright, and funny. Crowds cheered him at every stop. He would lash out at the Republican Congress, calling it "the worst in my memory," and accuse Republicans of being more interested in "the welfare of the better classes" than in the welfare of ordinary people. "Give 'em hell!" people would cry out. "I'm going to," Truman would say, "I'm pouring it on and I'm gonna keep pouring it on."

Truman also displayed a folksy quality that charmed audiences. "Howja like to meet my family?" he would ask, once his short speech was over. Then he'd introduce his wife Bess as "the boss" and daughter Margaret as "the boss's boss." Once the introductions were completed, Truman would lean over the rail to shake hands with

Democrat Harry Truman, an underdog in the 1948 election campaign,
used whistle stopping to help score a surprising victory.

those he could reach. He was usually still shaking hands as the train pulled out.

Dewey also tried campaigning by train, but he had far less success. He lacked Truman's warm and easygoing manner. And he sometimes made remarks that backfired. Once, in Beaucoup, Illinois, Dewey was speaking from the rear platform when the train gave a sudden lurch and started backing into the crowd. Although no one was hurt, Dewey declared, "That's the first lunatic I've had for an engineer. He probably should be shot at sunrise, but we'll let him off this time since no one was hurt."

Dewey's remarks about the poor engineer hurt him with voters. And Truman made the most of the incident. "We've had wonderful train crews all across the country," Truman said; "[they are] all Democrats." He added that Dewey "objects to having engineers back up. He doesn't mention that under that great engineer, Hoover, we backed up into the worst depression in history."

At another train stop, Dewey noted there were a great many children in the crowd and remarked that they should be grateful because he got them a day off from school. Then one kid yelled out, "Today is Saturday!" The crowd roared.

Truman's whistle-stop campaign enabled him to be seen by about six million Americans. How many voters were among them nobody knows for sure. But they helped Truman squeeze out a victory that stunned the experts.

Modern Whistle Stopping

In 1984, when President Ronald Reagan faced Walter Mondale, Reagan visited five Ohio cities aboard a thirteen-car train named the "Hawkeye Special." Reagan's staff did its best to re-create a miniature whistle-stopping campaign in the tradition of Harry Truman. They even arranged for the president to ride the "Ferdinand Magellan," the luxurious railroad car that Truman had used in 1948.

But times had changed. The antique car was equipped with modern communications equipment, which Reagan used to call the crew of the space shuttle circling overhead. Secret Service men lined the track and sought to conceal themselves in the bushes along the train's route. And when the 200-mile trip was over, television and newspaper representatives were whisked back to Washington, D.C. by airplane.

The Reagan campaign train was little more than a prop in a staged campaign event. It was meant to provide a focal point for the media and for stories about the size and enthusiasm of the crowds. David Hoffman, a White House correspondent for the *Washington Post,* noted, "It was quite clear that this was no Harry Truman train." Said Hoffman, "It was nothing like the time trains were used for genuine campaigning."

Radio and Politics

The high-tech equipment aboard the Reagan campaign train merely served to show the inadequacies of running for high national office by trying to appear *in person* before large numbers of voters. In the years following World War I, technology was providing devices that could carry a candidate's message to millions at the speed of light, and whistle stopping proved to be expensive, slow, and inefficient. The first such new device was radio. From its beginnings as an experimental gadget, radio developed into a dependable means of mass communication and, eventually, the largest mass medium in the world.

On November 2, 1920, station KDKA in Pittsburgh presented the nation's first previously announced radio broadcast. The historic broadcast announced the results of the voting in the election between Warren G. Harding and James M. Cox.

Radio grew enormously during the next few years. By 1922 there were 30 radio stations and 60,000 radio sets in the United States. Only five years later there were 733 stations and 7,300,000 sets.

In 1924, when Republican Calvin Coolidge faced Democrat John W. Davis, radio played a role, but the medium was still in its infancy. There were few regularly scheduled programs; there was no radio "network," no hookup of stations that would permit the same program to be broadcast across the whole country. The Republicans

Republican candidate Herbert Hoover prepares to speak into one of the cumbersome radio microphones of the day during a campaign stop in 1932.

broadcast from their own stations each day, transmitting Coolidge's speeches. Coolidge defeated Davis by about a two-to-one margin in both the popular and electoral vote. On March 4, 1925, the new president's inaugural address was carried by twenty-seven stations to an estimated fifteen million listeners.

At first, radio carried candidates' campaign speeches, and did little more than that. But little by little, candidates began to tailor their material to the medium. Candidates learned that they did not have to shout into the microphone. Radio demanded a more conversational style. There were strict time limits that had to be observed. In his final address of the 1928 campaign, Al Smith, the Democratic candidate, showed a deep understanding of the new medium when he told the audience, "Tonight I am not surrounded by thousands of people in a great hall and I am going to take this opportunity to talk intimately to my radio audience alone, as though I were sitting with you in your home and personally discussing with you the decision you are to make tomorrow."

Radio not only transformed political campaigning but significantly changed the perspective of the voters. Instead of attending or helping to organize rallies or parades, or gathering with friends at the town hall or public square to hear a candidate speak, people sat in their living rooms in twos and threes around a radio set to hear what candidates had to say. Americans were becoming mere passive "listeners."

Radio Comes of Age

Radio played a vital role in the 1932 presidential campaign, when Franklin D. Roosevelt was swept into office. Roosevelt's speeches attacking President Herbert Hoover were brief, interesting, and often dramatic. Each dealt with a single issue. And each was broadcast to millions of radio listeners. Roosevelt took part in countless motorcades and whistle-stop tours, but the radio messages reached a wider audience.

A feature of the campaign was Roosevelt's trek to the Pacific Coast and back again by train. It showed the candidate to be in high

Herbert Hoover, as secretary of commerce, participated in the first public demonstration of television in 1927. His voice and picture were transmitted over telephone wires from Washington, D.C., to New York City.

spirits and excellent health, despite an attack of polio in the summer of 1921. The more he campaigned, in fact, the more enthusiastic he seemed to become. Roosevelt's vigor and confidence contrasted sharply with Hoover and his radio voice, which often was tired and dreary.

It took until 1936, when Roosevelt was running for reelection, for the Democrats to pay off the radio debts they had incurred four years before. And the networks served notice that they did not intend to wait another four years to get paid for the bills the Democrats would run up in 1936; they demanded cash in advance.

Roosevelt avoided making payment by claiming, until the final weeks of the campaign at least, that he was speaking as president, not as a presidential candidate. He was thus entitled to free air time. The debate over whether a presidential candidate is speaking as the nation's chief executive or as an officeseeker has continued to this day. Now, of course, it is not so much the radio networks but the television networks that are involved.

Roosevelt also made clever use of radio as president. He scheduled periodic "Fireside Chats" with the American people, using them to introduce the broad economic and social reforms that made up his "New Deal." But Roosevelt was careful to explain his policies in very personal terms, always focusing on real people and dramatic events.

The Birth of Television

Even before radio reached its days of glory, television had arrived on the scene. On April 7, 1927, Herbert Hoover, secretary of commerce at the time, took part in the first public demonstration of television. His picture and voice were carried from Washington, D.C., to New York City.

In 1939 Franklin D. Roosevelt, presiding at ceremonies opening the World's Fair in New York, became the first president to use the medium to deliver an address. But there were only a few sets in use at the time, and Roosevelt's televised remarks reached fewer than 100,000 viewers.

The following year, 1940, the Democratic and Republican conventions were covered by TV, but the audience was still small. It was not until after World War II that television became an important factor in election campaigns. For the election of 1952, with eighteen million sets in use, a mass television audience was available for the first time. American politics would never be the same again.

CHAPTER FIVE

MASS APPEAL

The election of 1952 pitted General Dwight D. Eisenhower, the commander of Allied forces in World War II, against Adlai Stevenson, governor of Illinois, a man who combined obvious intelligence with a light touch. Eisenhower ran as a Republican, Stevenson as a Democrat.

In the amiable, easygoing Eisenhower, the Republicans possessed an enormously popular candidate. The slogan "I Like Ike" swept the country. For his running mate, Eisenhower picked young Senator Richard M. Nixon of California, a "gut fighter" known for his fierce crusade against the "Communist conspiracy."

Robert Montgomery, a noted motion picture and TV actor of the day, supervised Eisenhower's television appearances. Americans were captivated by the candidate's sunny smile, his charm and warmth. They saw him as a wise father who would keep the nation safe and secure.

At one early strategy meeting, Eisenhower's advisers talked so much about "merchandizing Eisenhower's frankness, honesty, and integrity" that it dampened the candidate's spirits. "All they talked about," he told a friend, "was how they would win on my popularity. Nobody said I had a brain in my head."

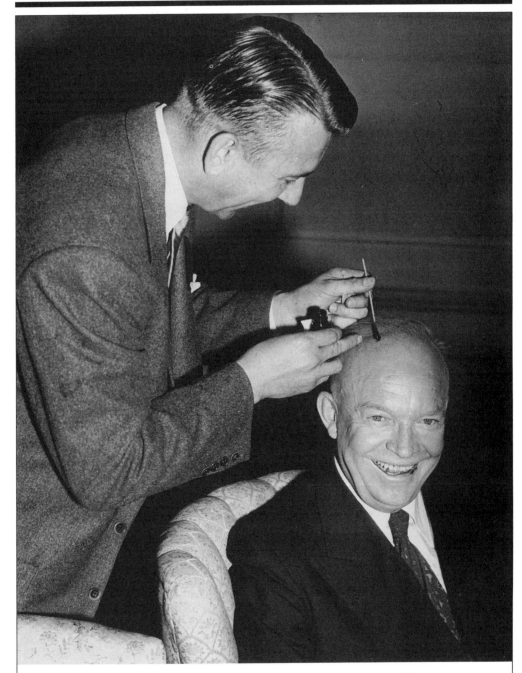

Republican candidate Dwight D. Eisenhower made skillful use of television in scoring a massive landslide victory in 1952. Here "Ike" is treated for a wound on his head in a TV studio on November 3, 1952. Eisenhower was injured when a clock, to be used as a prop, fell and hit him.

Television commercials were a major feature of the campaign. In one commercial, an announcer declared, "Eisenhower answers the nation." The scene quickly shifted to a man in the street, who asked, "Mr. Eisenhower, what about the high cost of living?" Eisenhower replied, "My wife, Mamie, worries about the same thing. I tell her it's our job to change that November 4th." In another commercial, a man asked which party would beat back inflation. Eisenhower answered: "Well, instead of asking which party will bring prices down, why not ask which party put prices up?"

To reach the largest possible audiences, both the Republicans and Democrats preempted top-rated television shows with speeches delivered by their candidates. This strategy once backfired on the Republicans. They purchased the time period of "I Love Lucy," the most popular show of the day. As Eisenhower's speech was being delivered, the network was flooded with telegrams of protest, many of which read: I LIKE IKE. BUT I *LOVE* LUCY. The Republicans did not buy the "Lucy" time period again.

Eisenhower campaigned more as an individual than as a representative of the Republican party, which, at the time, strongly opposed Communism and the Korean War. As a result, millions of Democrats "split" their ticket, that is, they made Eisenhower their choice for president, while voting for Democrats for other offices.

Democratic candidate Stevenson suffered from disclosures of corruption during the administration of Harry Truman and from the nation's growing discontent with the Korean War. Many people had the feeling that it was "time for a change."

Stevenson was an eloquent and effective speechmaker, but he had difficulty adapting his skill to the demands of television. He did not like the teleprompter, the device used to show a speaker an enlarged line-by-line reproduction of a script. He felt it was a barrier between himself and his audience, and he was never comfortable using the device. He preferred reading from typewritten pages. But when he looked down to read, the camera focused on the top of his bald head.

Stevenson was also hampered by a desire to write his own speeches. However, the demands of a modern campaign required an enormous number of speeches, some tailored to appeal to specific

Candidate Adlai Stevenson, an eloquent speaker, was unable to adapt his skills to the demands of television.

regions of the country, others to special interest groups; still others were designed to respond to current events or the accusations of other candidates. It was too much for one man, no matter how bright, to provide.

The "Checkers Speech"

Eisenhower's campaign got off to a slow start, but by mid-September, after he had brought hostile party factions together, things seemed to be working smoothly. Suddenly trouble flared. The problem concerned not Eisenhower himself, but his thirty-nine-year-old running mate, Richard Nixon.

On September 18, 1952, a blaring headline in the New York *Post* declared: SECRET RICH MEN'S TRUST FUND KEEPS NIXON IN STYLE FAR BEYOND HIS SALARY. According to the *Post*, sixty-six wealthy Californians had maintained a "slush fund" of more than $18,000 for Nixon during the time he served in the Senate. During the campaign, Nixon had been lashing out at the Democrats for their "scandal a day" administration. When Nixon admitted he had used the fund for political expenses, he and the Republicans found themselves involved in a scandal of their own.

The *Washington Post* and the New York *Herald Tribune* called upon Nixon to resign from the ticket. Many Republicans agreed. How could Eisenhower wage a campaign against corruption in government, they wanted to know, if his running mate was suspected of wrongdoing?

On Tuesday, September 23, at Eisenhower's suggestion, Nixon went on television to defend himself. At the time the highest-rated television program on Tuesday evening was the "Milton Berle Show." The Republicans purchased a half hour of network time for Nixon at 9:30 P.M., right after Berle.

Though Nixon claimed that he was "baring his soul" during the telecast, he did not reveal the names of those who had given him the money, nor did he tell exactly how it was spent. Instead, he defended the fund and in an emotional speech gave a detailed accounting of his personal finances. He spoke of his humble beginnings, his rise in life through determination and hard work, and the family's plain and simple life-style. He noted that his wife Pat did not have a mink coat. "But she does have a good Republican cloth coat," he said. He disclosed that he and his wife owed his parents $3,500 and paid interest on the loan "regularly."

He also talked about the family dog. "One other thing I should probably tell you," he said, "because if I don't they probably will be saying this about me too. We did get something, a gift, after the nomination. A man down in Texas heard Pat on the radio mention the fact that our two youngsters would like to have a dog and, believe it or not, the day before we left on this campaign trip we got a message from Union Station in Baltimore, saying they had a package for us. We went down to get it. You know what it was? It was a little cocker spaniel dog, in a crate that had been sent all the way from Texas — black and white, spotted, and our little girl Tricia, the six-year-old, named it Checkers. And you know, the kids, like all kids, loved the dog, and I just want to say this right now, that regardless of what they say about it, we are going to keep it."

Nixon's "Checkers speech," as it came to be called, was a huge success. In the days that followed, an estimated two million letters, cards, and telegrams in praise of Nixon poured into Republican headquarters. Eisenhower had no choice but to keep Nixon on the ticket.

The *New York Journal-American* described the speech as "magnificent." But to the New York *Post*, the newspaper that had broken the story of the secret fund, it was "a soap opera."

A few weeks later, the Eisenhower-Nixon ticket scored a tremendous victory, gathering 33,926,252 votes to 27,314,992 for Stevenson. It was the largest number of votes ever cast for a presidential candidate up to that time. In the electoral college, Eisenhower got 442 votes; Stevenson got 89.

Nixon, went on, in 1968, to become the nation's thirty-seventh president. He later acknowledged the significance of the Checkers speech. "If it hadn't been for that broadcast," Nixon wrote in his book *Six Crises,* "I would never have been around to run for the presidency."

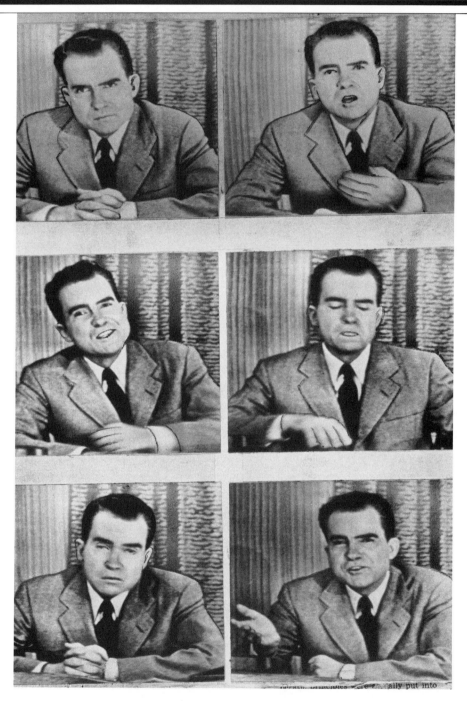

Richard Nixon's "Checkers speech" in 1952 worked to save his place on the Republican ticket.

Johnson versus Goldwater

The Checkers speech delivered by Richard Nixon in the 1952 campaign would come to typify how candidates would use television in the years that followed. They would do what Nixon had done: pay for the time and control the format. The more spontaneous format of interviews and press conferences would come to be looked upon as hazardous to one's political health. Instead, candidates came more and more to rely on commercials, televised speeches, and staged news events.

The power of television commercials was forcefully demonstrated in the 1964 presidential campaign, one in which voters were offered a choice between Barry M. Goldwater, the conservative Republican senator from Arizona, and Democrat Lyndon B. Johnson, who, as vice-president, had succeeded to the presidency late in 1963 following the assassination of President Kennedy. Johnson wanted to carry forward Kennedy's civil rights program. He also called for a "Great Society," in which every American would enjoy a high standard of living.

Goldwater spoke out against "crime in the streets" and "softness" on Communism. He had made some disturbing statements about American foreign policy. He wanted to break off diplomatic relations with the Soviet Union, get out of the United Nations, and use "low yield nuclear bombs," if necessary, in fighting the Communists in Vietnam and elsewhere. Goldwater also said he would like to "lob one into the men's room of the Kremlin and make sure I hit it."

Taking note of such statements, the Democrats sought to portray Goldwater as being impulsive, someone who would act without much thought or judgment. He was branded as "trigger happy" for his willingness to "shoot from the hip." Democratic advertising attempted to get across the idea that Goldwater was more likely than Johnson to start a nuclear war or to use nuclear weapons in an existing war. A print ad prepared by the Johnson forces depicted the mushroom cloud of a nuclear explosion, with a headline across the picture that read: GOLDWATER'S AMAZING PROBLEM SOLVER.

The Democrats also used television commercials to get this idea

Scenes from a 1964 Democratic television ad. This commercial — later called the "daisy ad" — helped to link Republican candidate Barry Goldwater to the possible use of nuclear weapons.

across. One of them, since known as the "daisy ad," ranks as one of the most controversial ads in the history of political broadcasting. The commercial begins with a little girl standing in an open field. The camera moves in close as she plucks petals from a daisy, counting the petals as she picks them. When the child's voice reaches "nine," a man's voice begins a countdown of its own, in reverse order. In contrast to the innocent voice of the child, the man's voice is ominous. At "zero," the child's face dissolves to a mushroom cloud that expands until it completely fills the screen. Then Lyndon Johnson's voice is heard: "These are the stakes. To make a world in which all of God's children can love, or go into the dark. We must either love each other or we must die."

With the first showing of the ad, the Republicans screamed in protest, demanding that it be withdrawn. Dean Burch, head of the Republican National Committee, filed a formal complaint with the Fair Campaign Practices Committee. "This horror-type commercial is designed to arouse basic emotions and has no place in the campaign," Burch declared. "I demand you call on the President to halt this smear attack on a United States Senator and the candidate of the Republican party for the presidency." The Democrats quickly ordered the ad off the air.

Although the commercial ran only once, it created so much turmoil that on the next night all three networks showed it on their nightly news telecasts. It was shown on commentary programs and described in the press and news magazines. As a result, millions of people were exposed to the commercial anyway.

The daisy ad was not the only TV commercial produced by the Democrats that sought to link Goldwater to the use of nuclear weapons. There were others, and they were widely used. Print ads carrying the theme ran in daily newspapers. VOTE FOR GOLDWATER AND GO TO WAR, proclaimed a bumper sticker.

Long before election day, the polls forecast a defeat for Goldwater, whom millions of Americans had come to fear. And the polls were right. Johnson scored a resounding victory, defeating Goldwater by close to 16 million votes (43,126,506 to 27,176,799). Johnson received 486 electoral votes; Goldwater, 52.

Controlling the Format

Ironically, it was the man who presented himself as a peace candidate who was drawn into a long and painful war in Vietnam. As antiwar protests mounted, public confidence in Lyndon Johnson waned, so much so that Johnson, in a dramatic televised speech, declined to run for the presidency a second time. The war had split and weakened the Democratic party, leaving an opening for the return of Richard Nixon as the Republican candidate in the 1968 election campaign. Nixon's opponent that year was Hubert Humphrey, the former Minnesota senator who was serving as Lyndon Johnson's vice-president.

"Without television, Richard Nixon would not have a chance. He would not have a prayer of being elected because the press would not let him get through to people. But because he is so good on television, he will get through despite the press. The press doesn't matter anymore." Those were the words of Frank Shakespeare, one of Richard Nixon's top advisers, as quoted by Joe McGinnis in his book *The Selling of the President.*

Nixon refused to debate Humphrey and held only a limited number of press conferences (as did Humphrey). One thing Nixon did do, however, was to appear in a series of ten one-hour panel shows, produced by members of his staff. The shows were tightly controlled from beginning to end.

The first was set in a studio in Chicago. The panel consisted of two local newspaper reporters, one from Chicago, the other from Moline, Illinois, and six area residents. There was a studio audience of three hundred people, all of whom were selected by the local Republican organization. Members of the press were not permitted in the studio itself, but shunted off to an adjoining room where they watched the proceedings on a television monitor. The show's moderator was Bud Wilkinson, a close friend of Nixon and a former University of Oklahoma football coach. When Wilkinson introduced Nixon, the audience broke into loud cheers and applause. Although the show produced some revealing moments, the questions asked by the panelists were seldom tough ones. Nixon's responses were scarcely newsworthy.

A grinning Richard Nixon meets the media during his successful 1968 campaign for the presidency.

When the show ended, the audience streamed out of their seats, as it had been instructed to do, and surrounded Nixon. The last thing the home viewer saw was Nixon in the midst of a swarm of fans.

Presidential campaigns of the present day are based on the lessons learned during the campaigns of Richard Nixon, Lyndon Johnson, John Kennedy, and Dwight Eisenhower, all of whom depended on television, spending tens of millions of dollars on the medium.

Candidates have learned that the catchy thirty-second commercial is an effective means of influencing voters and trashing opponents without having to discuss issues in detail, thereby revealing one's ignorance or weaknesses, or committing oneself to a policy that can be carefully scrutinized. Candidates try to isolate themselves from reporters and to guard against offhand remarks or unprepared responses. Events are staged for their visual impact.

In public opinion polls, voters say that they want to hear discussions of the issues. But judging by the campaigns, the candidates do not seem to believe the voters really mean it.

CHAPTER SIX

PRESIDENTIAL DEBATES

In 1960 the Democratic presidential candidate, John F. Kennedy, a senator from Massachusetts, faced two problems. He was considered, at forty-three, too young to be president. And despite having served fourteen years as a Massachusetts representative and senator, he was said to be too inexperienced.

In an effort to overcome these drawbacks, Kennedy issued a challenge to his rival, Vice-President Richard M. Nixon, to debate on television. Kennedy wanted to show that there really was not much difference between himself and his rival in terms of age (Nixon was forty-seven), appearance, or their knowledge and understanding of domestic and foreign policy issues. Kennedy realized that even if Nixon refused to debate, he would "win," for Kennedy could then accuse Nixon of running away and depriving the American people of the opportunity to judge the candidates.

The challenge put Nixon, who was completing eight years of service as vice-president under Dwight D. Eisenhower, in a difficult position. He realized that if he said no, he would be judged fearful of his opponent. If he said yes, he would be giving Kennedy the opportunity to appear before millions of television viewers who now only knew that he was a good-looking senator from a rich family. Nixon accepted the challenge. He had debated Kennedy before, when both were members of the House of Representatives, and once in a meeting before a West Virginia civic group. And he had always done well. A star debater in high school and college, Nixon felt he had nothing to fear.

Nixon and Kennedy thereby established the tradition of face-to-face presidential debates before television cameras. Since then, debates have become an important and expected part of the election process. Watched by more than 100 million viewers, they have a strong impact on voters.

Nixon versus Kennedy

For those first televised debates in 1960, both Kennedy and Nixon prepared intensively. Campaign staff members and advisers grilled them with tough questions in mock debates before their televised appearances. A great deal of attention was paid to appearance and deportment, and to avoiding damaging or offensive remarks. The candidates finally met on September 26.

What struck viewers right away was the contrast in the two men's appearance. Kennedy was pleasant, vigorous, and assured, and gave the impression of being well informed in answering questions from a panel of newsmen. Nixon, who had recently been hospitalized with a knee infection, was pale, tired, and uneasy. A dark beard and a poor makeup job gave him a sinister look. Sweat trickled over his upper lip, making him look like a person under terrible stress.

Kennedy went on the attack right away, listing the failings of the Eisenhower administration. Nixon was adept in answering Kennedy, but his basic argument that he was more experienced than Kennedy and had "stood up" to Russian leader Nikita Khrushchev was not particularly exciting or dramatic.

Throughout the debate, Nixon addressed his remarks to his oppo-

The television studio at the time of the 1960 debates between presidential candidates Richard Nixon and John F. Kennedy. Their encounters established a tradition of televised debates.

nent. Kennedy, however, spoke directly to the television audience. This surely was one reason why those who listened to the debate on radio thought that Nixon did as well as, if not better than, Kennedy. But to the television audience, Kennedy was the clear winner.

There were three other televised debates during the campaign, but the first one had the greatest impact. It enabled Kennedy to make a favorable impression on tens of millions of voters. The Democrats produced a five-minute commercial from a tape of the first debate. The commercial showed Kennedy answering questions directly, factually, confidently. Nixon, in "reaction shots," sweated and scowled.

Pollster George Gallup predicted a close election, and he was right. In fact, it was the closest popular vote in American history. Kennedy's margin of victory was less than 120,000 out of nearly 69 million votes cast. In electoral votes, Kennedy won 303 to Nixon's

219. But had no more than 12,000 people in five states—Hawaii, Illinois, Missouri, Nevada, and New Mexico—voted for Nixon instead of Kennedy, Nixon would have obtained a majority of the electoral votes.

Political analysts still argue about just how influential those first debates really were. The first debate no doubt changed some votes, with Nixon backers crossing to Kennedy. The number was not great, however. Polls by the Roper organization indicated that 6 percent of the public—some 4 million voters—based their voting preference in 1960 on the debates. Of these votes, Kennedy won the support of 72 percent. Kennedy probably would have won many of these votes anyway. But if only the tiniest fraction switched from Nixon to Kennedy as a result of the first debate, it was enough, considering Kennedy's paper-thin margin of victory.

Ford versus Carter

After the Kennedy-Nixon confrontation in 1960, debates were not conducted for several elections. The risks were perceived as too great. A candidate might throw everything away with a chance remark, or the wrong color suit, or some mannerism that did not come across well on the television screen. In 1964, when President Lyndon Johnson opposed Barry Goldwater, Johnson declined to debate his opponent, and won an easy victory. In 1968, when Richard Nixon ran against Hubert Humphrey, Nixon showed no enthusiasm for debating, and won. Running for reelection in 1972, Nixon sidestepped George McGovern's challenge to debate, and won again. There was no evidence that televised debates were anything but trouble for candidates. One could lose an election in a debate, but how much could one gain?

It became a common tactic for the incumbent president to avoid debating. It simply did not make sense to offer a less-well-known challenger the chance to address 100 million television viewers.

In 1976, however, Gerald Ford, the incumbent president, issued a challenge to Jimmy Carter to debate. Ford really had no other choice. He had not been elected by the people. He had been chosen to serve as vice-president by Richard Nixon, with the consent of Congress, when Nixon's original vice-president, Spiro Agnew, was forced to resign because of accusations of tax fraud. Later, when Nixon himself left office under threat of impeachment for covering up the Watergate break-in, Ford moved into the White House.

These were not strong credentials for a popular victory at the polls. Ford had only complicated matters when he pardoned Nixon for Watergate-related crimes before there had been any trial.

There were three debates. In the first, Ford did well. He was cool and confident and looked very presidential. Carter was nervous and defensive from the outset. After the debate, he began to slip in the polls.

In the second debate, Ford stumbled. Max Frankel of the *New York Times* asked Ford a question about the Soviet sphere of influence in Eastern Europe. "There is no Soviet domination of Eastern Europe," Ford declared, "and there never will be under a Ford administration."

Frankel seemed stunned. He said: "Did I understand you to say, sir, that the Russians are not using Eastern Europe as their own sphere of influence in occupying most of the countries there, and making sure with their own troops that it's a Communist Zone?"

"I don't believe, Mr. Frankel," Ford answered, "that the Yugoslavians consider themselves dominated by the Soviet Union. I don't believe that the Rumanians consider themselves dominated by the Soviet Union. I don't believe that the Poles consider themselves dominated by the Soviet Union. Each of these countries is independent, autonomous, it has its own territorial integrity and the United States does not concede that those countries are under the domination of the Soviet Union."

Ford's advisers shuddered in dismay. What their candidate had said bore no relation to the facts. The headlines the next day confirmed the Ford camp's worst fears. He had committed a world-class blunder. What made it even worse was that it took Ford a week to concede that he had made a mistake. During that time, his words continued to be front-page news. His campaign never really recovered. Carter registered a narrow victory.

In 1976 President Gerald Ford (right) made a serious blunder in debating Jimmy Carter, the eventual election winner.

Carter versus Reagan

In 1980 there were three candidates for the presidency: President Jimmy Carter, a Democrat; Republican Ronald Reagan, and John Anderson, running as an independent. A debate was scheduled for all three, but Carter refused to take part, saying that Anderson was "primarily a creation of the press."

Ruth Hinerfeld, president of the League of Women Voters, the organization sponsoring the debate, announced that there would be an empty chair on the stage in Carter's place. A political cartoonist pictured it as a baby's high chair to underscore Carter's childish attitude toward the debate. Comedian Johnny Carson asked, "What if the chair wins the debate?" In the end, the idea of having an empty chair was dropped and Reagan and Anderson debated each other.

Carter eventually agreed to debate Reagan, but he may have regretted doing so. A slip of the tongue seriously damaged his campaign. When the discussion turned to arms control, Carter said, "I had a discussion with my daughter Amy the other day, before I came here, to ask her what the most important issue was. She said she thought nuclear weaponry and the control of nuclear arms." Carter's advisers were stunned. By involving young Amy Carter with such a serious issue, Carter had made it seem unimportant, and implied that he took the advice of children on matters of foreign policy.

From that evening on until the end of the campaign, Carter was ridiculed for what he had said. ASK AMY signs began to appear at Republican rallies. Reporters joked about a book entitled *Prospects for Nuclear Disarmament,* by Amy Carter. Reagan himself got into the act. He was in Milwaukee to deliver a speech when the crowd began to chant, "Amy, Amy, Amy." Reagan said sarcastically, "I know he touched our hearts, all of us, the other night. I remember when Patty and Ron were little, tiny kids, we used to talk about nuclear war."

Carter and Reagan debated only once during the campaign. Both men prepared carefully for the debate. Reagan appeared calm and self-assured, but Carter was less at ease and often sounded preachy. Reagan's confidence may have stemmed from an edge he had. In 1983 it was revealed that Reagan's campaign manager had obtained President Carter's briefing book just before the debate. The advance knowledge of Carter's strategy and what he planned to say helped Reagan prepare for the debate. Reagan called the incident "much ado about nothing," but later promised to fire anyone found guilty of wrongdoing.

Reagan versus Mondale

In 1984 Reagan ran for reelection against former vice-president Walter F. Mondale. The incumbent president was seventy-three years old at the time, and more than a few people wondered about his ability to serve four more rigorous years in the White House.

Reagan added to this speculation in the first of two television debates with Mondale. At one point, his mind seemed to go blank. When he summed up his positions at the program's end, he rambled. The next day, the *Wall Street Journal* featured this front-page head-

Seventy-three-year-old Ronald Reagan (left) joked about his age in televised debates with Walter Mondale in 1984.

line: IS THE OLDEST U.S. PRESIDENT NOW SHOWING HIS AGE? REAGAN DEBATE PERFORMANCE INVITES OPEN SPECULATION ON HIS ABILITY TO SERVE. Though Reagan himself was disappointed with his performance, he tried to laugh it off. "If I had as much makeup as [Mondale] had," said Reagan, "I'd have looked younger, too."

In the second debate, Reagan redeemed himself, performing with ease and assurance. He even made some jokes about the age issue. "I will not make age an issue in this campaign," he said. "I'm not going to exploit for political purposes my opponent's youth and inexperience."

On election day the Reagan-Bush ticket swept the nation. Reagan won 59 percent of the popular vote. In the electoral vote, he carried every state except Mondale's home state of Minnesota and the District of Columbia. The count was 525 electoral votes to 13. It was a stunning victory.

Debate Reform

The first debates held during the 1988 presidential campaign, which pitted Vice-President George Bush against Massachusetts governor Michael Dukakis, was hailed by the Baltimore *Sun* as "the best presidential debate in history." It was, said the newspaper, "the most substantial and least trivialized." David S. Broder of the *Washington Post* agreed, writing that the debate "did what debates are supposed to do. It did not decide the election but it sharply clarified the choice voters have to make."

Although debates have been acclaimed for providing voters with information and insight, few people doubt that they can be improved. There are not enough of them, say the critics. They start too late in the campaign and they do not reveal enough about the candidates or their policies.

One proposal suggests four prime-time debates, the first scheduled right after Labor Day. Each debate would focus on a single topic: one each on economic policy, foreign policy, and social issues, and one for whatever specific issues developed during the campaign.

Another suggestion for improving the debates concerns the way in which they are structured. In recent elections, a panel of reporters, acceptable to both candidates, questions first one candidate and then the other. Each candidate is given time to reply to his opponent. Critics say that this is not a real debate, but more like two press conferences going on at the same time. These critics question the need for a panel of reporters, an audience, or any time limit on the candidates' remarks. Such restrictions often permit a participant to escape from an uncomfortable situation.

An alternative format might allow the two candidates to meet face-to-face and directly address and question one another. A moderator would introduce subjects, clarify differences, and keep things under control. In Canada in the fall of 1988, Prime Minister Brian Mulroney and his challenger, John Turner, held such a debate. "They moved quickly and dramatically to impassioned argument," reported the *New York Times*.

The debates in 1960 were sponsored by the television networks

ABC, CBS, and NBC. In 1976, 1980, and 1984 the League of Women Voters served as sponsor. In 1988 the Commission on Presidential Debates, an organization started by the Democratic and Republican national committees, took over debate sponsorship. Since the parties are permanent political institutions, and have the allegiance of the candidates, they get respect. If the Commission on Presidential Debates recommends a particular number of debates, with a certain date and location for each, the candidates are likely to agree. Most observers agree that party sponsorship of the debates is a good thing.

CHAPTER SEVEN

RUNNING AND WINNING

On Election Day in 1984, Ronald Reagan scored the greatest landslide victory in the history of American politics, just as the polls had predicted. Reagan received 54,281,858 popular votes, or 59 percent of the total, badly defeating Walter F. Mondale. Reagan won every state but Mondale's home state of Minnesota and the District of Columbia, and won in the electoral college by a margin of 525 to 13. Reagan's popular vote was 6 million votes more than the number Richard Nixon, the previous record-holder, had received in 1972. The percentage of total votes cast for Reagan placed him alongside the top winners of the past—Warren G. Harding in 1920, Franklin D. Roosevelt in 1936, Lyndon B. Johnson in 1964, and Nixon in 1972.

"Reagan is the most popular figure in the history of the United States," said Speaker of the House, Democrat Thomas P. "Tip" O'Neill, right after the election. "No candidate we put up would have been able to beat Reagan this year." O'Neill was undoubtedly right. Reagan had profited from the fact that inflation, rampant under his predecessor, Jimmy Carter, had been checked. Voters believed that they were better off than they had been four years before.

And Reagan, a former actor, also benefited from his skill as a performer. He succeeded in projecting the image of a strong and gallant leader. He had convinced millions of Americans that the nation "stood tall." A vote for Reagan was seen as a vote for America.

Every presidential candidate seeks the kind of victory Ronald Reagan achieved in 1984. But it is not easy. Many factors are involved in the success of a campaign.

A major factor often not given the attention it merits is personal energy. "You must emerge bright and bubbling with wisdom and well-being, every morning at eight o'clock just in time for a charming and profound breakfast talk, shake hands with hundreds, often literally thousands of people, make several inspiring 'newsworthy' speeches during the day, confer with political leaders along the way and with your staff all the time, write at every chance, think if possible, read mail and newspapers, talk on the telephone, talk to everybody, dictate, receive delegations, eat . . . and ride through city after city on the back of an open car, smiling until your mouth is dehydrated by the wind, waving until the blood runs out of your arm, and then bounce gaily, confidently, masterfully into great howling halls, shaved and all made up for television with the right color shirt and tie . . ." That is how Adlai Stevenson described the demands of campaigning after his loss to Dwight D. Eisenhower in the presidential election of 1952. Campaigning is becoming ever more frantic and brutal.

One reason is because party loyalty is less important than it used to be. Many voters, young voters in particular, do not identify with either of the major parties. They might vote Republican in one election, Democratic in the next. As a result, candidates are less likely to be able to count on big blocs of votes that existed simply because groups of voters invariably supported one party over the other.

In recent decades, issues have become more important than party identification. Millions of voters make their decisions on the basis of

Democratic presidential candidate Adlai Stevenson's energy and charm are captured in this 1952 campaign poster.

how the candidates stand on several issues of deep concern to them. Candidates have been expected to explain how they would reduce the budget deficit and control inflation, or protect the environment, or curb crime and attack the drug problem.

Much depends on the specific circumstances of the campaign and how an individual candidate responds to them. In 1988 George Bush attacked Michael Dukakis as a big-spending, soft-on-crime liberal. Dukakis did not respond effectively to what Bush was saying until the last two weeks of the campaign because he thought Bush's charges were so wide of the mark that no one would be influenced by them. Dukakis lost.

Building an Organization

Today a presidential campaign requires what amounts to a well-organized army of political workers. A candidate needs staff members, consultants, and unpaid volunteers who will wage contests in fifty states and the District of Columbia simultaneously. A professional staff may include as many as five hundred men and women, and a candidate may call upon more than a million volunteer workers.

A campaign director heads the organization. He or she is in charge of strategy and tactics and supervises campaign workers. When George Bush ran for president in 1988, James Baker, a Houston lawyer and close friend of Bush, ran his campaign. Smooth and shrewd, Baker had directed Bush's first try for the presidency in 1980 and had served as Ronald Reagan's White House chief of staff. After Bush's victory, Bush named Baker secretary of state.

A media director is also essential. The media director supervises advertising and publicity and handles relations with television and the press. A pollster is needed to take public opinion surveys. Each candidate also needs a fund-raiser, treasurer, and comptroller. A coordinator of volunteer operations is needed. During the campaign, volunteers distribute leaflets, prepare mailings, solicit votes by telephone, and perform many other jobs. These unpaid workers are essential to every campaign. When a candidate travels, he needs

Volunteers prepare campaign fliers at the headquarters of Democratic presidential candidate Michael Dukakis in New York in 1988.

"advance people" to prepare the site and make certain there is an audience. A security chief works with local police to assure the candidate's safety.

Finally, a candidate needs a national headquarters, a center of operations. In recent elections, candidates have established their headquarters on one or more floors of downtown office towers in major cities. The offices are filled with rented or borrowed furniture. Why buy furniture when it is needed only for three months?

One section of the headquarters is given over to banks of telephones. Volunteers are also busy at computers that link the headquarters with field offices in other cities. Cardboard cartons containing campaign literature are stacked to the ceilings. Campaign posters decorate the walls. It is seldom quiet. Visitors and prospective volunteers crowd the reception area. Telephones never stop ringing. Workers come and go around the clock.

Winning the Party's Support

Once nominated, the candidate takes control of the party's national committee. The national committees of the Republican and Democratic parties each consist of two persons—a man and woman—for each state and the District of Columbia. The national committee conducts state voter registration drives, organizes fundraising operations, and does some polling.

The state and county parties play a critical role in the election. The Democratic and Republican parties are organized from the neighborhood level up. The smallest party subdivision is the precinct. There are 188,432 precincts nationwide. Each precinct contains almost a thousand voters. Each has its own voting machines or ballot boxes, its own list of registered voters, and a corps of election officials.

It is at the precinct level that party workers know the voters and seek to get them to the polls to vote for their party's candidate. Each candidate must energize these local party workers by campaigning for local candidates, helping to raise funds for them, and supporting issues and causes that are locally popular. Without a determined effort on the part of precinct workers, no campaign can hope to succeed.

Only the Republicans and Democrats are organized in each state on a precinct-by-precinct basis. Other parties may put forth candidates in presidential elections, but, in reality, most elections are a contest between Democrats and Republicans. In fact, since 1860, there have been only four presidential elections in which the combined vote for all third, or minor, parties came to more than 10 percent of the total vote.

Developing a Theme

A candidate must develop a campaign theme, a statement that expresses his or her principal message to the voters. In 1988 George Bush won by running as the candidate of continuity, not change. The Republican theme was that a vote for Bush was to be a vote for the continued peace and prosperity of the Reagan years.

An incumbent president often runs on themes of peace and prosperity. That is what Ronald Reagan did in 1984 when he faced Walter Mondale. "America's back," said a Reagan TV commercial. "People have a sense of pride they never thought they'd feel again."

A candidate who is challenging an incumbent president usually argues that "it's time for a change." When Ronald Reagan ran against President Jimmy Carter in 1980, one of Reagan's television commercials asked: "Can we afford four more years of broken promises? In 1976, Jimmy Carter promised to hold inflation to 4 percent. Today it's 14 percent. He promised to fight unemployment. But today there are 8½ million Americans out of work. He promised to balance the budget. What we have is a $61 billion deficit. Can we afford four more years?"

Using the media, principally television, each candidate's theme is projected to every household in the nation. For the three months the campaign lasts, the candidates try to appear on television every night.

Though candidates often try to avoid committing themselves on specific issues, and use code words and slogans to describe where they stand, it would be wrong to assume that political campaigning is all fluff. A candidate's principal theme and the phrases and language he or she uses *do* "get through" to the voters. They come to understand that a particular candidate puts a strong defense ahead of domestic spending, for example, or that another believes economic considerations should temper our rush to clean up the environment, or that still another believes a little more unemployment is preferable to more inflation. For the public record, of course, no candidate favors guns instead of butter, or dirty air or unemployment, but the slogans and the phrasing of a candidate's principal theme often tell the electorate more than a candidate will admit to.

A Numbers Game

Considering the winner-take-all structure of the electoral college, the first rule in developing campaign strategy would seem to be clear: concentrate on California, New York, Texas, and other states with big electoral-vote totals. It does not make much sense to spend a great deal of time campaigning in Nevada, Vermont, Wyoming, or other states with just a handful of electoral votes.

On the other hand, what is the point of campaigning in California if polls there tell you that your opponent is going to win the state? There is no need to campaign or spend money there. A candidate's time can be used to greater advantage elsewhere. So the basic strategy has to be modified: The candidate must campaign in those doubtful states having the most electoral votes. A "doubtful" state is one that either candidate might win.

What every candidate hopes for is a group, or bloc, of states that can be counted on. Between 1932 and 1944, the Democrats, with Franklin D. Roosevelt as their candidate, won stunning victories partly because a cluster of Southern states traditionally supported Democratic party programs and candidates. The region came to be known as the "Solid South." Democrats could also count on votes from the industrial North in those years.

Times have changed. In the past fifty years, there has been a dramatic shift in population, with millions of Americans migrating from the Northeast to the South, Southwest, and West. Traditionally Democratic states have shown a big drop in electoral votes. At the same time, states that have been traditionally conservative and Republican have gained in electoral strength. Between 1932 and 1990, for example, New York's electors have dropped from 47 to 38. During the same period, the number of electors in California and Florida more than doubled.

Political scientist William Schneider, writing in the *Atlantic*, pointed out that in 1932 the Northeast and Middle West accounted for 54 percent of the nation's electoral votes; the South and West accounted for 46 percent. By 1990 those figures had been reversed. Because they now outnumber Democrats in the South, Southwest, and West, Republicans have come to have a built-in advantage in recent presidential elections. This situation does not guarantee a Republican victory, but based on election results over the past twenty years, the Republican candidate starts out with approximately 200 electoral votes.

Horace W. Busby, who once worked for President Lyndon Johnson, developed the theory that the Republicans have a "lock" on the electoral votes. Says Busby, "To refer to these campaigns as 'races' misses the point. In reality, one party starts off right next to the finish line."

Campaign Strategy

One of the most important concepts in developing campaign strategy is targeting. Through targeting, campaign strategists choose the people at whom the campaign message will be aimed. Areas of possible strength or weakness are studied through computer analysis. Economic and social conditions and the age, income, and geographical distribution of people are considered. Information is extracted from previous election results and public opinion polls.

"Candidates spend a lot of time talking with the 'wrong' people," says one campaign consultant. "They talk to people who aren't registered to vote. They talk to people who are registered but don't intend to vote in the election. And they talk to people who have already made up their minds." Targeting helps the candidate direct his or her efforts to the "right" people — registered voters who can be persuaded to come out on election day and vote for the candidate.

Part of the strategy of winning an election requires appealing to the ethnic, racial, and religious loyalties of special groups. Such groups have figured prominently in politics from the beginning.

Blacks, for example, identify closely with the Democratic party. Since 1964, blacks have given 85 percent of their votes to Democratic candidates. It is logical, then, for a Democratic candidate to make a special appeal for black votes. Hispanics in the Northeast also tend to be heavily Democratic. Cuban-Americans in Florida, however, favor the Republicans. Among religious groups, Jews are traditionally Democratic. Republicans count on support from white Protestants in the North who are of English, Scottish, Welsh, Scottish-Irish, or German descent.

Re-elect President
F. D. ROOSEVELT
FOR PRESIDENT

Franklin D Roosevelt

★羅斯福總統對於中國政見

一　尊重中國主權獨立，領土完整。
二　維持門戶開放政策。
三　不承認滿洲偽國。
四　實行中美兩國攜手親善，經濟合作。
五　推進中美商人來往待遇平等。
六　廢除苛例。
七　優待中美航空路線。
八　擴大中美商業。

★政府撥款防備旱災新政策，動用大宗欽項，其作用如下。可以節省政府之將來救災費用。同時可以恢復實業原狀。改良婦女工作時間。

一　救濟失業工人政策。
二　保護家庭提高婦女生活程度。
三　建設機會充分之民主政治。
四　救濟一切在苦難中之男婦老幼。
五　蓋吾人所奮鬥者不僅為拯救吾人之男婦老幼。不僅為經濟上之貧困。亦為民主政府。亦為拯救全

★世界之生存之民治政體。
★凡有選舉權者請於十一月三號選羅斯福總統復任。
★美國民政黨中央黨部全國競選委員會美籍華人部編

Chinese-American Division
DEMOCRATIC NATIONAL
CAMPAIGN COMMITTEE
Hotel Biltmore
New York
303

There's nothing new about seeking votes from ethnic minorities. This handbill dates to Franklin Roosevelt's campaign for reelection in 1944.

As women have become increasingly important in national and local politics, candidates seek to appeal to them. In recent elections, a majority of women have identified more closely with the Democrats than with Republicans. In 1980, for example, when Ronald Reagan opposed President Jimmy Carter, Reagan was said to be suffering from a "gender gap" because a majority of women supported Carter.

George Bush's Strategy

Just before Memorial Day weekend in 1988, five of Vice-President George Bush's top advisers traveled to Paramus, New Jersey, for what may have been the most important strategy session of his campaign for the presidency.

The weekend meeting in Paramus was called because Bush's aides were becoming uneasy. A new Gallup poll had just put Bush 16 percentage points behind his rival, Massachusetts governor Michael S. Dukakis. Even worse, the same survey showed that while about an equal number of voters liked Bush as disliked him, there was no such uncertainty about Dukakis. Five voters liked Dukakis for every one who did not, according to the poll.

Bush's advisers realized that something had to be done quickly. Although it was several months to election day, if the public continued to be charmed by Dukakis, this could be a serious problem later on. The members of the Bush high command arranged for two groups of fifteen voters each to be used in a "market test" of "pitches" they had been storing in campaign computers.

Hidden behind a two-way mirror, the Bush aides—who included campaign manager Lee Atwater and media consultant Roger Ailes—watched as the panel of voters were given information about Dukakis. They were told about Dukakis's veto of legislation that required teachers to lead their classes in the Pledge of Allegiance, and about pollution in Boston Harbor. They were also given information about a prison furlough program in Massachusetts, and were told how Willie Horton, a convicted murderer, had left the state on one of his weekend leaves of absence, traveled to Maryland, and

One of George Bush's campaign commercials pictured criminals passing through a "revolving door" of Michael Dukakis's Massachusetts prison system.

there assaulted a couple in their home, raping the woman.

At the start of the session, all thirty panel members supported Dukakis. At the end, only fifteen did. The Bush team realized it had the material it needed to defeat Dukakis in the fall election. From that point on, the 1988 presidential race set a new low in the use of negative ads. Saying bad things about one's opponent became the order of the day. It was a campaign of mocking attacks and personal blows.

The Bush forces sought to show that Dukakis was soft on crime, that he was the criminals' candidate, by telling the Willie Horton story over and over again in television commercials. Groups of Bush supporters arranged publicity tours for Horton's victims. Bush himself referred to Horton's story whenever he could.

Few people stopped to consider that the Massachusetts furlough system was not unusual. Every state has a furlough program of one type or another, and many involve convicted drug dealers and murderers. Sometimes the furloughs are for a day; other times they are for a weekend. In the federal prison system, a furlough can be as long as a month.

Some television commercials were based on half-truths or even outright lies. A TV ad produced by the Bush team showed a pool of sludge and pollutants near a sign reading DANGER/RADIATION HAZARD/NO SWIMMING. A voice blamed Dukakis for failing to clean up Boston Harbor. But the sign shown in the commercial had nothing to do with Dukakis and what he may or may not have done regarding the environment. The sign was meant to warn Navy personnel not to swim in waters where nuclear submarines under repair had once docked.

The Democrats were guilty of distortion too. One Dukakis ad accused Bush of casting a "tie-breaking Senate vote to cut Social Security benefits." In truth, that never happened. What Bush had done was to vote to eliminate a cost-of-living adjustment in benefits. He had not voted to reduce the actual amount of anyone's check.

Unfortunately, negative ads are popular with candidates because they often work. They are a tradition that goes back at least 150 years, to 1840, when the supporters of William Henry Harrison, the log cabin candidate, gossiped that his opponent, Martin Van Buren, dressed in women's corsets and doused himself with cologne. Harrison won.

Theodore Roosevelt was alleged to be a drunkard and drug user. It was whispered that Woodrow Wilson was, by the end of his presidency, hopelessly insane, and that Franklin Roosevelt was a secret Jew whose name was Rosenfelt. There were also rumors that Roosevelt was mentally ill. There were said to be bars on all the White House windows above the second floor to prevent the president from flinging himself out.

What is different about negative campaigning today is that, in the past, accusations about candidates were usually merely whispered, or were the subject of rumor or cheap handbills. Today it is part of the mainstream. Virtually every candidate seeks to "go negative."

One solution to negative campaigning in television ads might be what the *Washington Journalism Review* has called the "truth cure." The candidates' political commercials would be analyzed by the press on evening news telecasts. Commentators would turn the spotlight on any inaccurate statements, misleading claims, or false implications.

Early in 1990, when former San Francisco mayor Dianne Feinstein and California attorney general John Van de Kamp, both competing for the Democratic nomination for governor of California, began pounding one another on radio and television with charges and countercharges, area journalists decided to take a closer look. The campaign's first negative ad, aired by the Van de Kamp forces, drew the attention of the *Los Angeles Times*. "The Van de Kamp attack takes some liberties with the record of Feinstein," the *Times* article said. A comparison of the ad with Feinstein's actual record ran alongside the article.

Later in the campaign, Feinstein ran a picture of Richard Nixon in a local newspaper and sought to link Van de Kamp to Nixon's record as a negative campaigner in California, when he ran for the Senate in 1950. The *Los Angeles Times* called the Feinstein ad "particularly nasty." The *San Francisco Chronicle,* the *Sacramento Bee,* and other papers also analyzed the candidates' commercials.

"Those of us who are in the business of producing political media are on notice that we have to be more careful," said Bill Carrick, one of the producers of Feinstein's ads. Nevertheless, negative and even dishonest campaigning does influence voters. Candidates simply would not engage in such tactics if they did not profit from doing so. It will require a stronger negative reaction from a more discerning American public before such tactics disappear.

CHAPTER EIGHT

MONEY, MONEY, MONEY

During 1990, Vaclev Havel, a playwright, former political prisoner of the Communists, and newly elected president of his native Czechoslovakia, visited the United States. Addressing a joint session of Congress, Havel impressed his listeners with his intelligence and eloquence. After the speech, a reporter for the *New York Times* asked Representative Bill Thomas of California, a frequent critic of American politics, how the thoughtful and enlightened Havel might fare in an election in the United States. Thomas replied: "How much money does he have?"

In politics today, money is indeed the key. It does not matter whether a person is running for a local office such as mayor, or a seat in Congress, or the presidency; huge sums of money are needed.

In the case of the presidential election, money is often what separates the serious contender from those who drop out during the primaries. The quest for cash continues during the general election campaign. In 1988 both Michael Dukakis and George

Niagara Frontier Citizens for McGovern
651 Main Street, Buffalo, N. Y. 14203
I support Senator McGovern in the effort he is launching to lead the Democratic Party and our country along the path of peace, reconciliation, and rededication. Enclosed is my contribution of:

☐ $5 ☐ $10 ☐ $25 ☐ $100 ☐ $ ....

☐ I want to work for McGovern. Call me ....

☐ Mr.
☐ Ms. _____

Address _____

City _____ State _____ Zip _____

Occupation _____ Business Address _____

A copy of our report filed with the appropriate supervisory office is (or will be) available for purchase from the Superintendent of Documents, United States Government Printing Office, Washington D.C. 20402.

During the presidential election campaign of 1972, George McGovern's supporters sent out requests for contributions like the one shown here.

Bush crisscrossed the country seeking big money at fund-raising dinners and other such events. "Money is the mother's milk of politics," says one observer. "A baby needs milk to grow. A politician needs money to conduct a winning campaign."

Campaign Financing

In 1974 amendments to the Federal Election Campaign Act created the Presidential Election Campaign Fund. It provides for taxpayer financing of presidential election campaigns.

Every federal income tax form provides a place for a taxpayer to voluntarily earmark one dollar of his or her taxes toward this campaign fund. About one-third of all taxpayers support this fund. The money is used to "match" whatever money is raised by the candidates, up to a certain limit. It is not just Democrats and Republicans who benefit. Candidates representing minor parties are also eligible for a share of federal funds. A minor party is defined as one that receives from 5 to 25 percent of the popular vote in the preceding presidential election.

In 1988 Michael Dukakis and George Bush each received $46.1 million in public money to run their campaigns. In order to qualify for this money, each had to promise to forego all private fund-raising and abide by a spending ceiling. But they did not. Each candidate took advantage of loopholes in the campaign laws to raise another $50 million. This money is usually referred to as "soft" money. Critics of the system call it "sewer" money.

Soft money is channeled through state political parties rather than national campaign committees, and the local organization is permitted to spend unlimited amounts on "party building" and voter registration in presidential election years. There are no limits on how much money can be raised. Early in 1988 the Republican party released the names of 249 contributors, each of whom had given $100,000 or more in soft money to the Bush campaign. Officials for the Bush campaign claimed that the $100,000 contributions were for "party building" activities, and did not violate the laws covering campaign financing.

Soft money often goes to nominally independent groups that do not have to meet federal spending requirements, but which in reality remain under the control of campaign officials. In the 1988 presidential election the Dukakis campaign in Illinois was run by a committee called Campaign '88, an offshoot of the state party. Though the official Dukakis campaign office in the state had only 5 employees, Campaign '88 employed about 115 workers. George Bush and the Republicans operated in similar fashion in Texas and other states. Actual campaign committees were kept small. State parties were assigned to handle field operations. The *New York Times* called such evasions "brazen cheating."

Political Action Committees

Although limits have been set on how much one corporation or one union can contribute to a candidate, such institutions are still able to donate large sums of money through political action committees, or PACs. A political action committee is a group of people with a common goal who join together to raise funds for candidates who are in a position to affect their particular interests. Political action committees are formed by labor unions, business organizations, and others.

Since the PAC, in theory at least, is an issue-oriented, nonpartisan group not controlled by a political party, it would be very difficult to forbid such groups from raising money to fight for their causes. The money they receive and the way in which it is spent is not coordinated with the expenditures of a candidate's own election committee. Noncoordinated campaigns are protected by the First Amendment of the Constitution. To limit them would be an infringement on freedom of speech. Some PACs, however, are thinly disguised partisan groups raising money for a particular candidate, and others are obviously trying to buy a candidate's support for a particular issue. For these reasons, PACs have come in for much criticism.

"Dear Voter"

Another important tool used by candidates to raise money and win votes is called direct mail. It consists of letters, brochures, and postcards sent to large numbers of people.

Pieces of direct mail, delivered by your local letter carrier, arrive at your home or apartment almost every day from companies that want to sell your family something. These companies do not send out letters at random. They target potential customers by renting mailing lists from companies that sell related products. If you subscribe to *Sports Illustrated,* you've probably received direct mail from the *Sporting News* asking you to become a subscriber. If you've ever ordered a CD, cassette, or record by mail, you have no doubt heard frequently from music clubs who want to sign you up as a member.

The same technique is used in politics. Direct mail consultants target certain groups of voters and launch appeals to them. They begin by compiling mailing lists. A consultant for a conservative candidate might purchase the subscription list of the *National Review,* a magazine known for its support of conservative causes. A liberal candidate would be interested in obtaining the subscription list of *The Nation,* a liberal-minded publication. Mailing lists are also

The Watergate hotel and apartment complex in Washington, D.C., gave its name to the scandal that led to President Nixon's resignation.

purchased from labor unions, professional groups, and other organizations. For instance, a person who has donated money to the American Cancer Society is likely to be interested in health issues, and would be a target for the appropriate direct mail message. A person who belongs to the National Wildlife Federation is almost certain to be interested in environmental issues. Direct mail pieces are used both to raise funds and to influence citizens' opinions — and, ultimately, their votes.

Watergate

The rules and regulations that govern, or fail to govern, campaign spending today can be traced to June 17, 1972. On that day five men were arrested for breaking into the national headquarters of the Democratic party at the Watergate complex of apartment and office buildings in Washington, D.C. The men had tried to place taps on two telephone lines and photograph documents.

One of the five burglars was James W. McCord, Jr., the security coordinator for the Committee to Reelect the President (CREEP). The five men, along with G. Gordon Liddy, a CREEP aide, and E. Howard Hunt, Jr., a White House consultant, were indicted for a number of crimes, including burglary and wiretapping. In January 1973, five of the seven, including Hunt, pleaded guilty. The two others were found guilty by a jury.

Washington Post reporters Carl Bernstein and Bob Woodward investigated the break-in, and produced evidence that White House officials had tried to use the Central Intelligence Agency and the Federal Bureau of Investigation to impede the police inquiry. These officials falsely claimed it was a national security matter.

The Justice Department appointed Archibald Cox, a Harvard law professor, as a special prosecutor to handle the case. At about the same time, a select committee of the U.S. Senate opened televised hearings, and John W. Dean, a former White House counsel, became a vocal witness against Nixon in the hearings. Dean said that he had played a key role in a White House cover-up and charged that Nixon knew of his activities. Ultimately, seven officials of the Nixon administration were indicted on charges of conspiracy in covering up the break-in. Former attorney general John Mitchell and two of Nixon's top aides, John D. Ehrlichman and H. R. Haldeman, were each convicted of conspiracy, obstruction of justice, and perjury. They would receive prison terms of one to four years.

When the Senate learned that Nixon had secretly made tape recordings of White House conversations, committee members subpoenaed the tapes to answer questions raised during their investigation. Nixon refused to furnish the committee with certain tapes, and agreed only to provide written summaries. Archibald Cox said the summaries were not acceptable. Nixon ordered his attorney general to fire Cox. The attorney general resigned in protest. When the deputy attorney general also refused, Nixon fired him too. Events had reached a boiling point. In October 1973 a number of members of the House of Representatives took steps to begin impeachment proceedings.

On July 24, 1974, the House Judiciary Committee adopted three articles of impeachment for consideration by the full House of Representatives. The first accused Nixon of obstruction of justice. The other two articles involved abuse of power, that is, misuse of the CIA, FBI, and also the Internal Revenue Service to harass political opponents.

Nixon's defenders continued to argue that he had committed no impeachable offenses. But on August 5, 1974, Nixon turned over transcripts of taped conversations and other evidence to the federal district court judge who was trying the Watergate cases. One tape revealed that Nixon had conspired with his closest aides to cover up White House involvement in the Watergate crisis as early as June 23, 1972 — only six days after the break-in. What support Nixon had in Congress collapsed. He resigned on August 9, 1974, and Vice-President Gerald Ford took office as president that same day.

Reforming Campaign Financing

Watergate did not begin as a scandal about campaign financing, but as more and more documents were examined by Congress and prosecutors, a disturbing pattern of financial manipulation began to emerge. During the investigation, for example, it was disclosed that the Justice Department had entered into a settlement of an antitrust suit against the ITT Corporation shortly after an ITT subsidiary, the Sheraton Corporation, agreed to supply $400,000 worth of services to the Republican party for its 1972 national convention in San Diego.

Nixon's fund-raisers also went through the files of government regulatory agencies in search of cases involving large corporations. They would meet with officials of those corporations, bring up the cases, and request contributions.

In 1972 the Amerada Hess Corporation, a New York-based oil company, faced an Interior Department investigation of its refinery operations in the Virgin Islands. Leon Hess, the company's chief executive officer, contributed $250,000 to the Nixon campaign. Soon after, the Virgin Islands' investigation was ended.

Such abuses triggered major changes in how presidential campaigns were to be financed. In 1974 Congress approved amendments to the Federal Election Campaign Act of 1971 that provided for public financing of presidential campaigns and established the Federal Election Commission (FEC) to enforce the rules.

But the reforms that Congress legislated have not prevented private individuals, or corporate or union officials, from making big contributions to presidential campaigns. The Federal Election Commission lacks enforcement power, and gets only limited financial support from Congress. As a result, candidates have no fear of the Federal Election Commission. "Any good election lawyer can show you how to get around virtually all of the campaign finance laws," said Carol C. Durr, the chief legal counsel for the Dukakis presidential campaign organization.

The members of Congress themselves and their special interests loom as a roadblock to financing reform. PACs give more money to Democrats, who control Congress, than to Republicans. Thus, Democrats are not eager to rewrite the rules regarding PACs. Limits could be placed on contributions made to state organizations for party building and registration. But Republicans in Congress benefit the most from this soft money. Thus change in this area is not likely to occur any time soon.

During the early 1990s, calls for reform became louder and louder. Most voters believe that there must be a better way to finance elections, but there is a lack of will among politicians in Congress to change existing laws or formulate new ones.

CHAPTER NINE

PREDICTING ELECTION RESULTS

The 1988 presidential election campaign between George Bush and Michael Dukakis was not noteworthy merely because it was the most negative campaign in three decades. It was also the subject of the heaviest polling ever undertaken. In the months leading up to the election, voters were besieged with almost daily reports—on television, in the newspapers, and in national magazines—of public opinion polls that attempted to gauge the level of support for each of the candidates. The *New York Times* estimated that "news organizations conducted nearly twice as many national surveys this year as in the 1984 general election."

The pollsters did very well in 1988. They all correctly predicted the winner and most ended up with estimated voter percentages that were quite close to the actual results. There were variations, however. One national poll showed Bush with a 4 percent lead; another had him ahead by 11 percent. The actual results were 54 percent of the popular vote for Bush and 46 percent for Dukakis, a difference of 8 percent. "The pollsters did a strong job this time," wrote the *New York Times.* "Given the nature of polling, the national polls get about as close as you can get."

About 95 percent of all political surveys are done by telephone, according to Neil S. Newhouse, vice-president of the Wirthlin Group, a major polling firm. The phone numbers are selected at random. That means that each household with a telephone has an equal chance of being selected. "Most national public opinion polls interview anywhere from 800 to 1,500 people for their surveys," says Newhouse. "Although this may not seem like a lot, if the people are chosen randomly from across the country, they do represent a statistically valid cross section of Americans."

Polls are widely criticized because they focus too much attention on who is winning and who is losing. This is horse-race polling. The voters get numbers that do not help them make a decision on the basis of important issues. "We've bred a group of political writers who can't write a story without a poll," I. A. Lewis, polling director of the *Los Angeles Times,* told the *Washington Journalism Review.* "It's the same with campaign managers. You call one and say, 'How's your guy doing?' He says, 'I don't know. I don't have a poll.'"

Too great an emphasis on polling is not the only problem. More and more, the question is being asked: Do the polls sway the voters by suggestion?

Some observers believe that when the polls place one candidate far ahead of another shortly before election day, it discourages those who support that candidate from voting. Why bother? they say. If a candidate has an election all sewn up, an extra vote is not needed. Conversely, if the polls report that one candidate has a huge lead, voters for the opposing candidates may not feel that it is worth the effort to cast a ballot.

As yet, however, no clear-cut evidence has been put forth to suggest that, despite all the attention poll results get from the media, voters are influenced by them. There are probably as many voters who want to back the underdog in an election as those who want to support a clear winner.

Looking Back

Polls are not a new device. A survey of public opinion was taken as early as 1824 by the Harrisburg *Pennsylvanian.* The newspaper asked voters in Wilmington, Delaware, to name their preferences in the presidential election that year. On the basis of its poll, the newspaper predicted that Andrew Jackson would defeat his three opponents. Though Jackson won in the popular voting, he did not get a majority of the electoral votes, and John Quincy Adams won the election. Still, the poll was an accurate one.

The Gallup organization, founded by George H. Gallup, is the oldest firm using scientific methods to determine who voters are likely to choose in a presidential election. Gallup took his first survey in 1936 and found out, as other pollsters also would, that election polls can be an excellent way to attract publicity.

But polling and pollsters had some difficult days before attaining the reputation they now enjoy. In 1936 the magazine *Literary Digest* sent out some ten million questionnaires concerning the presidential election held that year. Two million questionnaires were returned. On the basis of those replies, the magazine predicted that Alfred M. Landon would defeat President Franklin D. Roosevelt. Roosevelt won. It was later determined that the *Literary Digest* poll was wrong because its questionnaires were mailed to people who were listed in telephone directories or in records of automobile ownership. The sample was not an accurate cross section because, in the middle of the Great Depression, only the well-to-do had telephones and cars.

In 1948 pollsters were wrong again, predicting that Governor Thomas E. Dewey of New York would trounce President Harry Truman. Truman won in a stunning upset. It is now believed that the last polls in 1948 were conducted too long before election day, and many voters changed their minds.

It was not until the 1960 presidential campaign between John F. Kennedy and Richard Nixon that polling became popular and respected again. Though the election of 1960 was very close, the Gallup organization correctly called the result. The same year, poll-

Franklin D. Roosevelt's stunning election victory in 1936 went unseen by pollsters representing Literary Digest.

ster Louis Harris won widespread recognition for the private polling he conducted for Kennedy, the election winner.

While techniques have improved enormously since the 1960s, voters are still capable of surprising the pollsters. In 1980 Ronald Reagan won a landslide victory over Jimmy Carter, but the polls failed to predict it. On November 3, 1980, the day before election day, a headline in the *New York Times* read: REAGAN AND CARTER STAND NEARLY EVEN IN LAST POLLS. On election day itself, the *Times* headline declared: RACE IS VIEWED AS VERY CLOSE. The next day, of course, the *Times* and other newspapers across the country had to report Reagan's runaway victory.

*Pollsters forecast New York Governor Thomas E. Dewey as th
winner in 1948. But Harry Truman (above) scored a memor*

Candidates' Polls

By the late 1970s most of the major news organizations, including the Associated Press, United Press International, and the three television networks, had developed the resources to conduct their own polls. The *Washington Post,* the *New York Times* and the *Los Angeles Times* joined in. Polls, they had found, were a wonderful device for capturing the attention of the public.

Presidential candidates also run their own polling operations. Polls help them plan their campaigns and keep track of their strength with the voters. In recent elections, pollsters have been important members of the campaign teams.

The pollster helps to make decisions that set the tone and direction of the campaign. In the 1980 and 1984 presidential campaigns, Richard Wirthlin was not only Ronald Reagan's pollster, but one of his leading strategists as well. Bob Teeter held a similar position with George Bush's campaign in 1988.

Candidates' pollsters are focusing more and more on tracking polls. A tracking poll measures voter sentiment on various issues on a day-to-day basis. Its chief purpose is to determine which groups of voters are moving toward or away from a candidate and why.

The question that is being asked more and more is how much poll results influence candidates. Do candidates change their positions on certain issues because of polling numbers?

Before polling became as sophisticated as it is today, candidates had little knowledge of how voters stood on particular issues. They depended on what they where told by party bosses. Today, with advances in research techniques, candidates know with a great deal of accuracy how voters feel.

Should a candidate come out strongly for gun control or should the issue be soft-pedaled? Should he or she support aid for Israel? How about environmental legislation? On such matters, the polling director is likely to dictate strategy and even influence what the candidate has to say.

Exit Polls

The 1988 presidential election officially ended on January 4, 1989. That was the day that Congress counted and certified the electoral college's ballots, and the results were announced by the vice-president (who happened to be George Bush, the election winner). But for most Americans, the election was over at 9:17 P.M. eastern standard time on November 8, 1988, the moment that CBS News projected George Bush the winner. Unfortunately, west of the eastern time zone, millions of Americans were still voting.

CBS, along with the other networks, made its forecast of the presidential winner on the basis of exit polls in various states. As voters left their polling places after casting their ballots, they were asked whether they had voted for Bush or Dukakis. The results enabled the networks to predict the outcome of the election.

Exit polls were first used by CBS in 1967 during a race for the governorship of Kentucky. They were not used to predict elections then, but simply as a means of getting more information for election night analysis. CBS used exit polls extensively during the 1968 presidential contest. The polls provided detailed information about how specific groups voted.

Exit polls are now a basic feature of election night coverage, used by all three networks. In 1988 the Cable News Network (CNN) began using them for the first time. But CNN used the polls for analyzing trends, not for projecting winners.

Exit polls have a bad name because they cause frustration and even anger among voters who are told, in effect, that the election is over before they have voted. Why should a person make the effort to vote if the television networks are saying the race is over? Exit polls and the projection of results on network television are often cited as one reason why only a little more than half of eligible voters go to the polls. It is not only the vote for the president that is affected. State and local races also suffer. And citizens on the Pacific coast feel that their vote counts only when a presidential race is very close.

Using information derived from exit polls, television networks have been criticized for forecasting election winners while polls in Western states are still open. Pictured above are Peter Jennings and David Brinkley of ABC-TV during the 1988 election-night broadcast.

The networks defend exit polls and their right to project election results whenever they please. Any restrictions, they say, represent suppression of the news. Dan Rather, the CBS news anchorman, said that he did not know whether the early projections discouraged those in the western states from voting. "I am told by our people that there is little or no evidence that projections hurt turnout," Rather said. "But common sense tells you they certainly could." Whether or not the projections affect voter turnout, Rather believes that voters have a right to know. "What doesn't make sense to me," said Rather, "is for us to know who the next president will be . . . but we just can't tell the people. We can't and won't do that."

Joseph Angotta, a vice-president at NBC News, said that the controversy put the network in a "no win" situation. "If we project before all the polls are closed, we get criticized," said Angotta. "If we wait for the polls in the West to close, large groups of critics will say we withheld information from the public."

An elaborate process is involved in taking exit polls. At NBC it begins with the selection of specific voting locations in all fifty states and the District of Columbia. At each of these sites, a random sample of voters is asked to fill out a questionnaire. It takes five or ten minutes, and the voters are not paid for their time or effort.

In all the states and in Washington, D.C., a total of 60,000 voters are asked which candidate they supported and why. The results are phoned to 300 operators at Cherry Hill, New Jersey, and typed into a computer for analysis. The data is then fed to NBC News headquarters in New York. If an exit poll for a state indicates that one candidate has been heavily favored in the voting, the network projects the candidate as the winner in that state. If the voting is close, the network will not announce a winner. If an exit poll for a state shows one candidate getting only 51 percent of the vote, and the other getting 49 percent, the race is judged too close to call. When that happens, NBC waits for voting results—real results—from sample precincts in the state. Sometimes even these numbers are not enough. The network also checks county voting results from the National Election Service, which is funded by the three networks, the Associated Press, and United Press International.

Giving Voters a Break

For years the networks continued to make use of exit-polling data to project the names of election winners. Though CNN and the Westinghouse Broadcasting Corporation, which owns many local television stations, were willing to withhold exit-poll information until after the polls had closed in a state, ABC, CBS, and NBC would not.

Early in 1985, however, the three networks changed their policies and joined the other two broadcasters. Each is now on record with a commitment not to use exit-poll data to suggest the probable winner in any state until the polls in that state have closed.

After broadcasters had made that commitment, exit polling itself was no longer a cause for concern. The problem was the availability of actual results from eastern states before the closing of polls in western states. Congress is attempting to solve that problem with uniform poll-closing legislation. If all polls closed at the same time, results in the East could not be used to indicate the outcome of an election while polls in the West were open.

The Uniform Poll Closing Bill, co-sponsored by Congressmen Al Swift of Washington and William Thomas of California, provides that polls in the eastern, central, and mountain time zones will close at 9:00 P.M. eastern standard time (which is 8:00 P.M. central standard time, and 7:00 P.M. mountain standard time). Daylight saving time will be extended for two weeks in the four- and one-half states that make up the Pacific time zone (Washington, Oregon, California, Nevada, and the Idaho panhandle). These states will be on daylight saving time on election day while the rest of the country is on standard time, and the polls in the Pacific time zone will close at 7:00 eastern standard time.

The Uniform Poll Closing Bill was passed by the House of Representatives early in 1990. It awaits action in the Senate.

CHAPTER TEN

WHO VOTES? WHO DOESN'T?

In the final days of an election campaign, workers for each of the candidates work hard to "get out the vote." They stand on street corners, knock on doors, and make telephone calls, encouraging anyone who has not registered to do so. They recommend the use of absentee ballots for those who cannot go to the polls. On election day, workers may even provide babysitting services for voters. In many areas, transportation to and from polling places is made available. Election Day is a legal holiday in most states in presidential election years. Many businesses shut down for the day, and schools close.

Despite the widespread recognition that voting is an essential part of good citizenship, millions of Americans stay home on election day. In fact, in the 1988 presidential election, only about half, 50.1 percent, of the voting-age population actually voted. That figure represented a drop of 12 percent since 1964, as the table on page 121 indicates.

Political observers agree that American democracy is being undermined by such voter indif-

President Ronald Reagan's total of 54,281,858 popular votes in 1984 was the biggest total in election history.

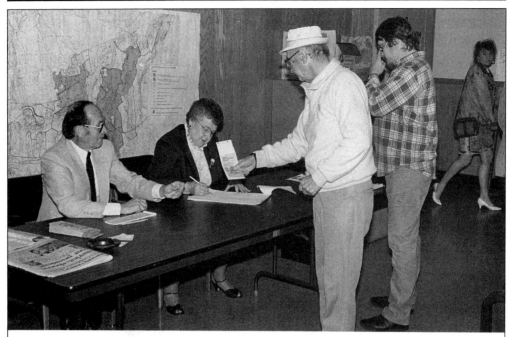

In Palmer, Massachusetts, voters are given their ballots to vote in 1988 presidential election.

ference. "American voters do not seem to understand their rightful place in the operation of democracy," declared the Markle Commission on the Media and the Electorate in 1990, following a two year study of presidential politics. "They act as if they believe that presidential elections belong to somebody else."

The Right to Vote

Voter participation has been declining despite the fact that more citizens are eligible to vote than ever before. During colonial times, only adult males who owned property had the right to vote. After the nation gained its independence, the Constitution gave the states the right to decide who could vote. One by one, the states did away with property ownership as a requirement for voting. By 1830 all white male adults could vote. Women and blacks were not permitted to vote until relatively recent times. These groups had to overcome strong opposition to gain their voting rights.

VOTES FOR WOMEN A SUCCESS

THE MAP PROVES IT

■ No Suffrage
▨ Partial Suffrage
⊡ Presidential Suffrage

Alaska—1913

WOMEN VOTE IN ALL THE WHITE STATES WHY NOT IN THIS STATE?

The Vote was given to Women in

Wyoming	1869		
Colorado	1893	Kansas	1912
Idaho	1896	Oregon	1912
Utah	1896	Alaska	1913
Washington	1910	Illinois	1913
California	1911	Montana	1914
Arizona	1912	Nevada	1914

Nearly 4,000,000 women vote in the Equal Suffrage States.
Total Number of Electoral Votes in Equal Suffrage States—91.

VOTE FOR WOMAN SUFFRAGE
GIVE THIS TO A FRIEND AND ASK HIM TO VOTE FOR IT

NEW JERSEY WOMAN SUFFRAGE ASSOCIATION
Headquarters: 309 Park Avenue, Plainfield   142
N. W. S. Publishing Co., Inc.

*American women didn't gain the right to vote until 1920. This is a
1914 suffragist handbill from New Jersey.*

Women began to agitate for the right to vote, or suffrage, as that right is called, during the mid-nineteenth century. In 1848 two women bent on reform, Lucretia Mott and Elizabeth Cady Stanton, called a public meeting in Seneca Falls, New York, where they drew up a Declaration of Sentiment patterned after the Declaration of Independence. It stated that men and women are "created equal," and it called for women to have equal rights in education, property, voting, and other matters. In 1869 the National Women's Suffrage Association was formed. Headed by Stanton and Susan B. Anthony, the organization sought an amendment to the Constitution that would give women the right to vote.

In 1869 the territory of Wyoming, recognizing that frontier women shared the same perils as men, gave women the right to vote.

But a constitutional amendment granting women suffrage was still a long way off. On March 3, 1913, the day before the inauguration of President Woodrow Wilson, thousands of women marched in a rally along Pennsylvania Avenue in Washington, D.C., in support of suffrage. Suddenly violence flared. Women marchers were slapped and kicked. Their banners were ripped from their hands. Soldiers had to be called to restore order.

In 1919 both Houses of Congress finally passed the Nineteenth Amendment to the Constitution, and by 1920 the required number of states had ratified it. The amendment reads: "The right of citizens of the United States to vote shall not be denied or abridged by the United States or by any state on account of sex." In the election of 1920, between Warren G. Harding and James M. Cox, women cast their votes for a president of the United States for the first time.

Black Americans struggled even longer than women to achieve the right to vote. Theoretically, blacks achieved voting rights in 1870, when the Fifteenth Amendment to the Constitution was ratified. That amendment stated that no citizen could be denied the right to vote "on account of race, color, or previous condition." But in practice, it took blacks much longer to win the vote. Most Southern blacks, having just emerged from slavery, could barely read or write, and some Southern states made the ability to read and write a requirement for voting. That destroyed the effect of the Fifteenth

Amendment. Poorly educated whites could not meet the literacy requirement, either.

Southern states also adopted "poll taxes," which had to be paid as a requirement for voting. Poll taxes, like literacy tests, prevented poor whites as well as poor blacks from voting. Some states then adopted "grandfather clauses," stating that anyone whose grandfather had been eligible to vote did not have to pass a literacy test or pay a poll tax. Since only the grandfathers of whites had voted, while the grandfathers of most blacks had been slaves, the vote was ingeniously returned to poor whites.

In 1915 the Supreme Court declared such grandfather clauses to be unconstitutional. And the Twenty-fourth Amendment to the Constitution, ratified in 1964, prohibited states from requiring citizens to pay a poll tax to vote in national elections. Two years later the Supreme Court banned the use of poll taxes in state and local elections as well.

In 1965, with the passage of the Voting Rights Act, the use of literacy tests was outlawed. Discrimination based on race or color was made a crime. The act also required ballots to be printed in two languages in any area where a significant number of people do not speak English as a first language. The Voting Rights Act was renewed in 1970 and 1975. In 1982 it was extended until the year 2007.

Amendments to the Voting Rights Act passed in 1970 lowered the voting age for national and state elections from twenty-one to eighteen. But the Supreme Court ruled that the law could apply only to national elections. In 1971 the Twenty-sixth Amendment to the Constitution lowered the voting age to eighteen for both national and state elections.

Registration

Registration, the process by which a person becomes eligible to vote, has also been used to restrict voter participation. Some states once required periodic registration. People had to register every year, or after some other designated period, in order to remain eligible to vote. Almost all states now have permanent registration.

The Commonwealth of Massachusetts
Office of the Secretary of State
Michael J. Connolly, Secretary
AFFIDAVIT OF REGISTRATION

FOR USE AT PETITIONED
OUT-OF-OFFICE SESSIONS ONLY

G.L. ch.51 § 42B

Please print all information

1. NAME _____
   Last   *First*   *Initial*

2. CURRENT ADDRESS _____
   House No.   Street Name   Apartment No.   City or Town   P.O. Box No.   Zip code

3. _____
   Residence January 1 (if different from above)

4. _____
   Last previous residence in another city or town, if any

5. _____
   Name used at this residence (if different from above)

6. DATE OF BIRTH _____   7. PLACE OF BIRTH _____
   Month   Day   Year   *City or Town   State   Country*

8. U.S. CITIZENSHIP   ☐ *By birth*   ☐ *Naturalized*   9. HEIGHT _____
                                                                  Feet   Inches

10. OCCUPATION _____

11. DO YOU WISH TO ENROLL IN A POLITICAL PARTY?   ☐ *Democratic*   ☐ *Republican*   ☐ *No (Independent)*

Please read carefully. I hereby swear (affirm) that I am the person named above, that the above information is true, that I am not a person under guardianship, that I am not temporarily or permanently dis-
qualified by law from voting because of corrupt practices in respect to elections, and that I consider this
residence to be my home. *(A copy of this document may be forwarded to the Department of Revenue and
the Registry of Motor Vehicles.)* Signed under the pains and penalties of perjury.

12. Registrant _____
    Signature
13. Witness _____
    Signature of Registrar or Assistant Registrar
14. Date _____   15. City or Town where session held _____
16. Proof of residence (if any) _____

500M 2-85-802861

HOME REGISTRAR'S COPY

The form used to register voters in the state of Massachusetts.

That is, in no state do you have to register before *each* election.
However, failure to vote for several years or in one or two general
elections in most states will result in removal of one's name from the
voting rolls. The voter must then re-register.

Election officials realize that registration is a key to voter turnout.
In the 1988 presidential election, 85 percent of those registered to
vote did so. During the 1970s and 1980s, some thirty-four states
passed laws that lowered the barriers to registration. Hours for
registration were lengthened. Offices were kept open in the eve-
nings and on weekends. More than half the nation's voters became
eligible to register by mail.

In Ohio a voter can now fill out registration forms that come in the
mail just like the monthly utility bills. Such forms are also available at
every public agency in the state. If you live in Ohio, you can even
register at any McDonald's simply by filling out a form printed on
your tray liner, and then mailing the form to the office of the secretary of state.

Registering to vote in New York's Chinatown.

During the presidential election of 1984, both the Democrats and Republicans spent a great deal of time and money in an effort to recruit new voters through registration campaigns. In the 1988 election, both parties spent less on national registration drives and instead focused their attention on getting members of ethnic minorities and other special groups registered.

Dropping Out

Although it has become easier to register and vote than at any other time in the nation's history, the percentage of voters who show up at the polls keeps shrinking. In most other democracies, some 80 percent or more of all voters vote in national elections. In the United States the number hovers around 50 percent. In state and local elections the percentage is even lower.

In the 1988 presidential election the United States had its lowest voter turnout since 1924. Turnout was down among almost every age, income, and ethnic group. It declined for every occupational group and among voters of every level of education. Among citizens between the ages of eighteen and twenty-four, only 29 percent of those eligible voted.

At the same time, campaign spending increased enormously. Curtis B. Gans, director of the Committee for the Study of the American Electorate, believes that these two factors—the tremendous increase in campaign expenditures (with the money devoted largely to television) and the decline in turnout—are closely linked.

Gans points out that negative and trivial ads are not new. "Nor," he says, "are present versions more outrageous than those for other elections." What is different, he adds, is the number of such ads. "Where such ads were once limited to the occasional campaign . . . or put on largely by independent . . . groups," says Gans, "they are now the staple for all campaigns."

Historian Arthur Schlesinger, Jr., is also critical of the role television plays. He says, "The rise of electronic media has an effect on draining content out of campaigns." And according to Senator John C. Danforth of Missouri, "It has locked candidates into ridiculous positions because only ridiculous positions can be compacted into thirty-second commercials.''

Changing Television's Role

To encourage voter participation, the Markle Commission has called for more broadcast time for political programming. The commission has recommended that Congress direct the Federal Communications Commission "to call upon the networks regularly to offer public service air time during presidential campaigns to educate the electorate.''

If free time were given to candidates or political parties, broadcasters would be about the only ones to suffer. As it is now, every presidential election sees the transfer of huge sums of money, much of it donated by the taxpayer, to the television networks and local stations.

The Markle Commission has also recommended four presidential debates. It would make participation in the debates a condition for a candidate to receive federal campaign money.

Others have suggested putting controls on or even banning political advertising on television. Curtis Gans says, "The United States is the only democracy in the world that does not, either by time or format, regulate its television political advertising.'' In Western Europe, the practice generally followed is to grant free broadcast time to each party or candidate, with certain rules as to what can be done with that time. In France, for example, a candidate can address the public or stage a discussion, using associates or a friendly interviewer. But filmed messages of the type familiar to American viewers are out. In addition to formal political broadcasts, interviews with candidates and debates are presented. The basic idea is to permit the voters to get to know the candidates and their thinking on the issues.

The system we now have is not working. It has triggered an "astonishing" indifference to elections, says the Markle Commission. It is essential to reverse the trend. It is often said that people who do not vote get what they deserve. The same thing is true of people who do not keep informed about the candidates or the issues.

On the other hand, voters joining together have the power to elect, or cast out, a president of the United States. They also can express their ideas on the direction the nation should be taking. America's future depends on America's voters.

Year	Candidates	Voter Participation (% of voting-age population)
1964	Johnson-Goldwater	61.9
1968	Humphrey-Nixon	60.9
1972	McGovern-Nixon	55.2
1976	Carter-Ford	53.5
1980	Carter-Reagan	54.0
1984	Mondale-Reagan	53.1
1988	Dukakis-Bush	50.1

POPULAR AND ELECTORAL VOTE FOR PRESIDENT 1789 – 1988

Year	President elected	Popular	Electoral
1789	George Washington	Unknown	69
1792	George Washington	Unknown	132
1796	John Adams	Unknown	71
1800*	Thomas Jefferson	Unknown	73
1804	Thomas Jefferson	Unknown	162
1808	James Madison	Unknown	122
1812	James Madison	Unknown	128
1816	James Monroe......................	Unknown	183
1820	James Monroe......................	Unknown	231
1824*	John Quincy Adams	105,321	84
1828	Andrew Jackson	647,231	178
1832	Andrew Jackson	687,502	219
1836	Martin Van Buren	762,678	170
1840	William H. Harrison..................	1,275,017	234
1844	James K. Polk	1,337,243	170
1848	Zachary Taylor	1,360,101	163

Year	President elected	Popular	Electoral
1852	Franklin Pierce	1,601,474	254
1856	James C. Buchanan	1,927,995	174
1860	Abraham Lincoln	1,866,352	180
1864	Abraham Lincoln	2,216,067	212
1868	Ulysses S. Grant	3,015,071	214
1872*	Ulysses S. Grant	3,597,070	286
1876*	Rutherford B. Hayes	4,033,950	185
1880	James A. Garfield	4,449,053	214
1884	Grover Cleveland	4,911,017	219
1888*	Benjamin Harrison	5,444,337	233
1892	Grover Cleveland	5,554,414	277
1896	William McKinley	7,035,638	271
1900	William McKinley	7,219,530	292
1904	Theodore Roosevelt	7,628,834	336
1908	William H. Taft	7,679,006	321
1912	Woodrow Wilson	6,286,214	435
1916	Woodrow Wilson	9,129,606	277
1920	Warren G. Harding	16,152,200	404
1924	Calvin Coolidge	15,725,016	382
1928	Herbert Hoover	21,392,190	444
1932	Franklin D. Roosevelt	22,821,857	472
1936	Franklin D. Roosevelt	27,751,597	523
1940	Franklin D. Roosevelt	27,243,466	449
1944	Franklin D. Roosevelt	25,602,505	432
1948	Harry S Truman	24,105,812	303
1952	Dwight D. Eisenhower	33,936,252	442
1956*	Dwight D. Eisenhower	35,585,316	457
1960*	John F. Kennedy	34,227,096	303
1964	Lyndon B. Johnson	43,126,506	486
1968	Richard M. Nixon	31,785,480	301
1972*	Richard M. Nixon	47,165,234	520
1976*	Jimmy Carter	40,828,929	297
1980	Ronald Reagan	43,899,248	489
1984	Ronald Reagan	54,281,858	525
1988*	George Bush	48,881,221	426

* 1800 — Elected by House of Representatives because of tied electoral vote. 1824 — Elected by House of Representatives. No candidate polled a majority. In 1824, the Democrat Republicans had become a loose coalition of competing political groups. By 1828, the supporters of Jackson were known as Democrats, and the J.Q. Adams and Henry Clay supporters as National Republicans. 1872 — Greeley died Nov. 29, 1872. His electoral votes were split among 4 individuals. 1876 — Fla., La., Ore., and S. C. election returns were disputed. Congress in joint session (Mar. 2, 1877) declared Hayes and Wheeler elected president and vice-president. 1888 — Cleveland had more votes than Harrison but the 233 electoral votes cast for Harrison against the 168 for Cleveland elected Harrison president. 1956 — Democrats elected 74 electors but one from Alabama refused to vote for Stevenson. 1960 — Sen. Harry F. Byrd (D-Va.) received 15 electoral votes. 1972 — John Hospers of Cal. and Theodore Nathan of Ore. received one vote from an elector of Virginia. 1976 — Ronald Reagan of Cal. received one vote from an elector of Washington. 1988 — Sen. Lloyd Bentsen (D-Tex.) received 1 electoral vote.

	Losing candidate	Popular	Electoral
1789	No opposition	—	—
1792	No opposition	—	—
1796	Thomas Jefferson	Unknown	68
1800	Aaron Burr	Unknown	73
1804	Charles Pinckney	Unknown	14
1808	Charles Pinckney	Unknown	47
1812	DeWitt Clinton	Unknown	89
1816	Rufus King	Unknown	34
1820	John Quincy Adams	Unknown	1
1824	Andrew Jackson	155,872	99
1824	Henry Clay	46,587	37
1824	William H. Crawford	44,282	41
1828	John Quincy Adams	509,097	83
1832	Henry Clay	530,189	49
1836	William H. Harrison	548,007	73
1840	Martin Van Buren	1,128,702	60
1844	Henry Clay	1,299,068	105
1848	Lewis Cass	1,220,544	127

	Losing candidate	Popular	Electoral
1852	Winfield Scott	1,386,578	42
1856	John C. Frémont	1,391,555	114
1860	Stephen A. Douglas	1,375,157	12
1860	John C. Breckinridge	845,763	72
1860	John Bell	589,581	39
1864	George McClellan	1,808,725	21
1868	Horatio Seymour	2,709,615	80
1872	Horace Greeley	2,834,079	—
1876	Samuel J. Tilden	4,264,757	184
1880	Winfield S. Hancock	4,442,030	155
1884	James G. Blaine	4,848,334	182
1888	Grover Cleveland	5,540,050	168
1892	Benjamin Harrison	5,190,802	145
1892	James Weaver	1,027,329	22
1896	William J. Bryan	6,467,946	176
1900	William J. Bryan	6,358,071	155
1904	Alton B. Parker	5,084,491	140
1908	William J. Bryan	6,409,106	162
1912	Theodore Roosevelt	4,216,020	88
1912	William H. Taft	3,483,922	8
1916	Charles E. Hughes	8,538,221	254
1920	James M. Cox	9,147,353	127
1924	John W. Davis	8,385,586	136
1924	Robert M. LaFollette	4,822,856	13
1928	Alfred E. Smith	15,016,443	87
1932	Herbert E. Hoover	15,781,841	59
1932	Norman Thomas	884,781	—
1936	Alfred Landon	16,679,583	8
1940	Wendell Willkie	22,304,755	82
1944	Thomas E. Dewey	22,008,278	99
1948	Thomas E. Dewey	21,970,066	189
1948	J. Strom Thurmond	1,169,021	39
1948	Henry A. Wallace	1,157,172	—
1952	Adlai E. Stevenson	27,314,992	89
1956	Adlai E. Stevenson	26,031,322	73
1960	Richard M. Nixon	34,108,546	219
1964	Barry M. Goldwater	27,176,799	52
1968	Hubert H. Humphrey	31,275,166	191
1968	George G. Wallace	9,905,473	46

Losing candidate		Popular	Electoral
1972	George S. McGovern...................	29,170,774	17
1976	Gerald R. Ford	39,148,940	240
1980	Jimmy Carter.......................	35,481,435	49
1980	John B. Anderson	5,719,437	—
1984	Walter F. Mondale	37,457,215	13
1988	Michael S. Dukakis	41,805,422	111

GLOSSARY

ballot   A device such as a sheet of paper on which voters mark their choice of candidates.

bandwagon   A political campaign that attracts an ever increasing number of supporters.

boss   A leader with great power within a political party; bosses often manipulate voting and elections.

candidate   An individual who seeks or is nominated for political office.

caucus   A meeting of small groups of party members for the purpose of deciding questions of policy or selecting a candidate for elected office.

conservative   A political point of view. Conservatives are generally traditionalists. They have a narrow view of what government can achieve. Conservatives are generally opposed to high taxes and big spending programs.

convention   A formal meeting of members of a party to nominate candidates to run for President or other political offices.

democracy   A government of, by, and for the people, who have the right to choose their leaders and establish policy.

direct mail   Mail from a candidate or party, usually consisting of letters, brochures, or postcards, that is sent to large numbers of people.

election   Organized voting to choose a candidate for office.

elector   The individual or individuals (electors) chosen by the voters to elect the President and Vice-President of the United States. Each state has a certain number of electors; the number is the same as the total of the state's senators and representatives.

electoral college   The body of presidential electors chosen in each state and the District of Columbia every four years to elect the President and Vice-President of the United States. To win a presidential election, a candidate must claim a majority of the electoral votes.

electoral vote   The vote cast by members of the electoral college.

electorate   A body of qualified voters.

exit poll   A poll taken of voters as they leave their polling places just after having voted. The results enable the TV networks to forecast the election winner.

Federal Election Commission (FEC)   A government commission established by Congress to watch over elections and see that they are fair. The FEC also keeps records on campaign contributions and investigates instances of wrongdoing.

flier   A political pamphlet or circular for mass distribution. Fliers are an important political part of any political campaign and are usually handed out by volunteers.

general election   A nationwide election involving most or all political parties and their foremost candidates.

grandfather clause   A clause in a state law saying that any person whose grandfather had been eligible to vote prior to 1867 would not have to meet certain voting requirements. Since the grandfathers of most blacks had been slaves prior to 1867, and thus were not eligible to vote, the grandfather clause meant that only whites could vote. Grandfather clauses were ruled unconstitutional by the Supreme Court in 1915.

impeachment The constitutional method of charging the president, or judicial officials, with high crimes or misdemeanors and of trying them for misconduct in office. The House of Representatives votes for impeachment; the Senate conducts the trial.

inauguration The formal ceremony, including the taking of the oath, that takes place at the beginning of a President's term of office.

incumbent A person already holding political office.

independent voter A voter who does not belong to a political party.

landslide An overwhelming political victory.

liberal A political point of view. Liberals generally look to the federal government to play an active role in solving social problems and regulating the marketplace. Liberals usually support such social welfare programs as unemployment insurance and antipoverty legislation.

local election An election involving city, county, or town offices.

major party The Democratic or Republican party.

majority A number that is more than half of the total number.

matching funds Money for a political campaign provided by the federal government or another source equal in amount to funds that come through private donations.

media   Television, radio, newspapers, magazines, and other means of mass communication; an important tool in present-day politics and political campaigns.

minor party   See **third party.**

National Committee   A group of people chosen by a political party that selects the national chairperson and helps that person run the party, including the making of plans for the next national convention. In the case of the Democratic and Republican parties, the National Committee consists of a man and woman from each state and territory, plus the District of Columbia.

national convention   The convention held every four years by a major party to nominate candidates for President and Vice-President.

nominate   To propose as a candidate.

party   A political group organized to support its principles and candidates for public office and ultimately to gain control of the running of the government.

plurality   In a contest of more than two candidates, the number of votes cast for the winner, when the winner is not able to claim a majority of the vote.

political action committee (PAC)   An organization formed to raise money to be donated to candidates.

politics   The art and science of gaining elective office; also, the activities and affairs of a political party.

poll   See **public opinion poll.**

poll tax   A fee charged by local officials as a requirement for voting. Poll taxes are unconstitutional as a result of the Twenty-fourth Amendment to the Constitution, ratified in 1964.

polls   The place where votes are cast in an election.

pollster   A person who takes a public opinion poll.

popular vote   The votes cast by the voters at large.

precinct   An election district in a city or town; the smallest local unit within the organization of a political party.

primary election   A preliminary election in which members of a party in a state vote to select delegates to the party's national convention. The delegates in turn cast their ballots for the voters' choice. Depending on the state, the primary election may also involve party members in a state choosing a candidate.

public opinion poll   A survey of a sample of the public to obtain information or record opinion.

register   The process of formally enrolling the name of a qualified voter with a precinct.

registered voter   A person who is eligible to vote by means of formally enrolling his or her name with a precinct.

representative   A member of the House of Representatives, the lower house of the United States Congress. Representatives are usually called congressmen or congresswomen. The number of representatives elected by each state is proportional to the state's population.

senator   A member of the Senate, the upper house of the United States Congress. Two senators are elected from each state.

soft money Contributions given to candidates, meant to be used for "party building" and voter registration, and which are not subject to restrictions on campaign financing.

sound bite A fragment of television videotape, usually nine or ten seconds in length.

spot A commercial, often thirty seconds in length, on television or radio.

suffrage The right to vote in a political election.

third party A party organized as an alternative to the two major parties; also called a minor party.

ticket The list of candidates offered by a party in an election; also called a slate.

ticket splitting To vote for candidates from different parties.

tracking poll A poll that measures voter opinion on a day-to-day basis.

unit rule A voting rule permitted by the Democratic party at its presidential convention from 1860 to 1968. Under unit rule, the entire vote of a state delegation had to be cast for the candidate preferred by the majority, even though a portion of the delegation members might favor another candidate.

volunteer A person who works for a party or a party's candidate without being paid; often volunteers are the closest link between a party and the voters.

FURTHER READING

Alexander, Herbert. *Financing Politics.* Washington, D.C.: Congressional Quarterly Press, 1981.

Black, Christine M., and Thomas Oliphant. *All by Myself: The Unmaking of a Presidential Campaign.* Chester, CT.: The Globe Pequot Press, 1989.

Blumenthal, Sidney. *Pledging Allegiance: The Last Campaign of the Cold War.* New York: HarperCollins, 1990.

Boller, Paul F., Jr. *Presidential Campaigns.* New York: Oxford University Press, 1984.

Colton, Elizabeth O. *The Jackson Phenomenon: The Man, the Power, the Message.* New York: Doubleday, 1989.

Germond, Jack W., and Jules Witcover. *Blue Smoke and Mirrors: How Reagan Won and Why Carter Lost the Election of 1980.* New York: The Viking Press, 1981.

Grimes, Ann. *Running Mates: The Making of a First Lady.* New York: William Morrow, 1990.

Hadley, Arthur T. *The Empty Polling Booth.* Englewood Cliffs, N.J.: Prentice Hall, 1978.

Jamieson, Kathleen Hall. *Packaging the Presidency: A History of Criticism of Presidential Campaign Advertising.* New York: Oxford University Press, 1984.

Jamieson, Kathleen Hall, and David S Birdsall. *Presidential Debates: The Challenge of Creating an Informed Electorate.* New York: Oxford University Press, 1988.

Kalb, Marvin, and Hendrik Herzberg. *Candidates '88.* Dover, Mass.: Auburn House Publishing Co., 1988.

Lichter, Robert S. *The Video Campaign: Network Coverage of the 1988 Primaries.* Washington, D.C.: American Enterprise Institute for Public Policy Research: Center for Media and Public Affairs, 1988.

McGinniss, Joe. *The Selling of the President.* New York: Penguin Books, 1988.

Modl, Tom, ed. *America's Elections: Opposing Viewpoints.* St. Paul, Minn.: Greenhaven Press, 1988.

Page, Benjamin I. *Choices & Echoes in Presidential Elections.* Chicago: University of Chicago Press, 1979.

Pious, Richard M. *American Politics and Government.* New York: McGraw Hill, 1986.

Polsby, Nelson W. and Aaron Wildavsky. *Presidential Elections: Contemporary Strategies of American Electoral Politics.* New York: The Free Press, 1988.

Pomper, Gerald M., et al. *The Election of 1988: Reports and Interpretations.* Chatham, N.J.: Chatham House Publishers, Inc., 1989.

Reinsche, J. Leonard. *Getting Elected: From Radio and Roosevelt to Television and Reagan.* New York: Hippocrene Books, 1988.

Robinson, Michael J. and Margaret A. Sheehan. *Over the Wire and on TV: CBS and UPI in Campaign '80.* New York: Russell Sage, 1984.

Rosenstone, Steven J. *Forecasting Presidential Elections.* New Haven: Yale University Press, 1983.

Samuels, Cynthia K. *It's a Free Country! A Young Person's Guide to Politics and Elections.* New York: Atheneum, 1988.

Schlesinger, Arthur M., Jr. and Fred L. Israel, eds. *The Coming to Power: Critical Presidential Elections in American History.* New York: Chelsea House, 1981.

Taylor, Paul. *See How They Run: Electing the President in an Age of Mediaocracy.* New York: Knopf, 1990.

Wayne, Stephen J. *The Road to the White House: The Politics of Presidential Elections.* New York: St. Martin's Press, 1987.

Will, George F. *The New Season: A Spectator's Guide to the 1988 Election.* New York: Simon & Schuster, 1988.

Wolfinger, Raymond E., and Rosenstone, Steven J. *Who Votes?* New Haven: Yale University Press, 1980.

ACKNOWLEDGMENTS

Special thanks are due Richard M. Pious, Professor of Political Science at Barnard College, Columbia University, New York, New York, for his careful reading of the manuscript and his thoughtful suggestions. He played a valuable role.

The author is also grateful to Curtis Gans, Director, Committee for the Study of the American Electorate; Ludwiga Barabas, Robert A. Taft Institute of Government; Grant Thompson, Executive Director, League of Women Voters of the United States; Janet Brown, Executive Director, Commission on Presidential Debates; Rich Boylan, Democratic National Committee; Donna S. Knecht, Republican National Committee; Mary Ternes, Washingtonia Division, Martin Luther King Memorial Library; Allan B. Goodrich, John F. Kennedy Library; Kathleen A. Strauss, Dwight D. Eisenhower Library; Susan Y. Elter, Franklin D. Roosevelt Library; Jim E. Detlefsen, Herbert Hoover Library; E. Philip Scott, Lyndon Baines Johnson Library; Kenneth G. Hafeli, Gerald R. Ford Library; Benedict K. Zobrist and George H. Curtis, Harry S. Truman Library; David J. Stanhope, Jimmy Carter Library; Mary Kloser, National Archives; KatherineL. Brown, Woodrow Wilson Birthplace; Wallace Finley Dailey, Houghton Library, Harvard University; Donna Yorke, ABC Television; Lydia Derrick, CNN; Congressman Al Swift; Francesca Kurti, TLC Custom Labs; John Devaney, Aime LaMontagne, Adriane Ruggiero, and Tim Sullivan.

PHOTO ACKNOWLEDGMENTS

AP/Wide World Photos: 10, 57, 59, 70. Board of Elections, Commonwealth of Massachusetts: 117. Capital Cities/ABC, Inc.: 108. Gerald R. Ford Library: 20, 73. Herbert Hoover Presidential Library-Museum: 52, 54. Lyndon B. Johnson Library: 64. Library of Congress: 29, 34, 38, 44. National Archives: 62, 75. National Park Services—Abbie Rowe; courtesy Harry S Truman Library: 105. New York Public Library Picture Collection: 47. Franklin D. Roosevelt Library: 42, 104. George Sullivan: 6, 12, 18, 22, 27, 31, 32, 40, 45, 80, 82, 87, 89, 93, 96, 108, 113, 114, 118. Harry S Truman Library: 49. *Washington Post;* reprinted by permission of the D.C. Public Library: 67. The White House/Michael Evans: 112.

INDEX

Eastern Europe, 72
Ehrlichman, John D., 98
Eisenhower, Dwight D., 56–63,
    67, 68, 79
Electoral college system, 13–
    25, 128
  allegiance of electors, 19–20
  breaking deadlocks, 19
  electoral votes, 14–16, 17–
    18, 18–19, 37, 40, 46,
    61, 65, 70–71, 75, 78,
    85–86, 103
  electors, 13, 14–15, 19, 20,
    21, 23, 85, 128
  problems, 17–19
  process of altering, 24–25
  winner-take-all, 16–17, 24–
    25
Electoral Commission of 1876,
    17–18
Ethnic groups, 86, 107, 113,
    115–116
Exit polls, 107–110, 128

Fair Campaign Practices
    Committee, 65
Federal Bureau of Investigation
    (FBI), 97–98
Federal Election Campaign
    Act, 10, 99
Federal Election Commission,
    10, 99, 128
Federalist Party, 30
Feinstein, Dianne, 91
Fifteenth Amendment, 115–
    116
Fireside Chats, 55

First Amendment, 95
Florida, 25
Ford, Gerald, 19, 20, 71–73, 98
Frankel, Max, 72
Front porch campaigning, 37,
    41, 45–46
Furlough programs, 88–90

Gallup, George (Gallup polls),
    70, 88, 103
Gans, Curtis B., 119, 120
Gold standard, 43
Goldwater, Barry M., 63–65, 71
Gorbachev, Mikhail, 9
Grandfather clause, 128–129
Great Society, 63

Haldeman, H.R., 98
Harding, Warren G., 43, 51,
    78, 115
Harris, Louis, 103–104
Harrison, Benjamin, 18–19
Harrison, William Henry, 32,
    33–36, 90
Havel, Vaclav, 92
Hayes, Rutherford B., 17–18
Hess, Leon, 99
Hinerfeld, Ruth, 73
Hoffman, David, 51
Homelessness, 9
Hoover, Herbert, 52–55
Horton, Willie, 88–90
Hosper, John, 21
House of Representatives, 14–
    15, 17, 19, 98, 110
Humphrey, Hubert, 16, 66, 71
Hunt, E. Edward, Jr., 97